THE TOFU TOLLBOOTH

A Directory of Great Natural & Organic Food Stores

COMPILED BY
Dar Williams

ARDWORK
PRESS

Compiled by Dar Williams

Book Design: Dar Williams and David Caputo
Typesetting: David Caputo at Radical Solutions, Ltd.,
Amherst, Mass. (413) 549-6969 with assistance from
Mazen Credi, Tod Fisher and Sarah Davis

Front Cover Design & Illustration: Katryna Nields
Back Cover Photo: Curry Rose Mills
Icons: Annie Moonsong, Amy Fincke, Katryna and Dar
Map Preparation: Annie Moonsong, Sarah Davis,
Tod Fisher, Mazen Credi and David Caputo
Promotional Assistance: Kathleen Kavarra Corr
Ardwork Logo: Jonathan Shambroom

To order more copies, call 1-800-TOFU-2-GO or send a check
for $8.95 per copy (includes postage) to **Ardwork Press**

ARDW●RK
P
 R   P.O. Box 814
  E | Northampton, MA
   S   01061-0814
    S

Printed on
Recycled Paper

WELCOME TO
THE TOFU TOLLBOOTH

Presenting **over 700 natural food store entries**, collected by musicians, students, wayfarers and rugged-outdoor-types across the country. We're happy to announce that health food stores aren't just bad cookies anymore! These stores are often their community bulletin boards, resources for alternative healing, and sources of abundant, gorgeous, organic produce.

In order to keep out the **MPTF** (More Pills Than Food) stores, we established a criterion requiring that stores sell **organic produce**. There are some indicated exceptions to this, depending on recommendation and/or location. If we've missed an awesome store or truly glitched something, please let us know at **Ardwork Press**. If you're a new store, congratulations! Give us a call or send us a postcard of regional splendor!

We've done everything we can think of to help you find these stores. Most stores have **directions, hours and symbol profiles**. Listings have less info but are usually stores that have no organic produce or belong to a chain with other stores in close proximity.

Have a wonderful trip. We were going to list some "Travel Tips," but collectively, we as travelers have done everything wrong at some point and still had a great time...OK, three quickies: join an auto club (membership pays for itself in one towing), keep a flashlight in the car, and **USE THIS BOOK!**

Fondly,

Dar Williams

This is for Earl Hanson, 1927-1993
I hope this helps, Earl.

Thanks To:
Jaimé Morton, Sarah Davis, Dena Marger, David Caputo, Gray,
Marian, Julie & Meredith Williams, Morty Berger, Dan Farley,
Barry Evans, The Nields, Curry Rose Mills, Jaje Shambroom,
The Billys, Lisa Wittner, David Seitz, Adam Rothberg, John Capen,
Pete Nelson, Heather Horak, Jack Williams, Don Cognoscenti,
Jon Svetkey, Don White, Lori Ambacher, Laurel George,
Jim Infantino, Eric Nauman, Deb Vandertamp, Suzanne Davis,
Anne Weiss, Michael Robinson, Judy Minor, Clurie Bennis,
Kate Bennis, Elizabeth Zimels, Corey Robin, Rachel Henderson,
James Sauli, Lisi Philips, Rob Laurens, Karl Sikkenga, Scott Alarik,
The Amsel Family, Dana Robinson, Heather Horak, Brett Perkins,
Patty McGill, Kathleen Corr, Jan Luby, Amy Fincke, Ed Koren,
Heidi Creamer, Maz & Tod, Shemaya Mountain Laurel,
and countless other folks who've helped me in my travels.

These resources were a terrific help, as well:
National Co-op Directory
by George Keller
Published by the Co-op News Network
Box 583, Spencer, WV, 25276 • (304) 927-5173

City Spirit: Publisher of **NY, NJ, CT and NM Naturally**
53 Wycoff Street, Brooklyn, NY, 11201 • (718) 834-9101
There are separate resource guides for each of the four states,
covering all sorts of holistic health territory. Give them a call
(and thanks, Betty from Human Bean, for the info)!

The Natural Yellow Pages & InnerSelf Publications
915 S. 21 Ave., #2A & 3A, Hollywood, FL 33020 • (305) 923-0730
Another resource guide similar to City Spirit. This one for eastern Florida.

Table of Contents

Key

DELI

PET FOOD

BAKERY

BEER/WINE

CAFE

**WHEELCHAIR
ACCESS**

JUICE BAR

BATHROOM

SALAD BAR

**WHEELCHAIR
ACCESSIBLE
BATHROOM**

COFFEE-TO-GO

*All Stores Have
Organic Produce*
Unless Otherwise Indicated

ALABAMA

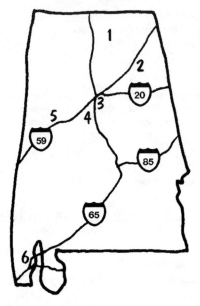

1. HUNTSVILLE
2. GADSDEN
3. BIRMINGHAM
4. HOOVER
5. TUSCALOOSA
6. MOBILE

BIRMINGHAM

GOLDEN TEMPLE NATURAL GROCERY
1901 11th Avenue South, 35205 • (205) 933-6333
M-F 8:30-7:30, Sat. 9:30-5:30, Sun. 12-5:30

I-65; from north: University Blvd. South exit. Turn right on 8th Ave.,
right on 19th Street. Store's at 11th Ave. on left. From south: 4th Ave.
South exit. Turn left onto 4th Ave, right on 19th St. Same as above.

GADSDEN

APPLE-A-DAY
280 North 3rd, in Gregerson's, 35901 • (205) 546-8458
*Apple-a-Day is a natural foods store in a 24 hour supermarket. Gregerson's has had
organic produce in its four stores (the others are in Aniston, Madison, and Russellville).
When you swing through Gregerson's, by all means ENCOURAGE them to keep it up!*
M-Sat. 8:30-8, Sun. 12-6

From I-59, take I-759 (spur), then 411 north.
Store's in the Midtown Plaza on left.

HOOVER
GOLDEN TEMPLE NATURAL GROCERY
3309 Lorna Road, 35216 • (205) 823-7002
Less organic produce than the other Golden Temple.
M-Sat. 10-6, Sun. 12-5:30

From I-65, take the Montgomery (Hwy 31) Hwy exit. From north: go
straight off exit ramp onto Lorna. Store's on left, 2-3 miles down. From
south: turn left on Hwy 31, then left on Lorna. Same as above.

HUNTSVILLE
GARDEN COVE PRODUCE CENTER
628 Meridian Street North, 35801 • (205) 534-2683
M-W 10-7, Th. 9-7, Fr. 9-3, Sun. 12-5

 From Memorial Parkway (Hwy 231), head
east on Pratt Street. Store's on right.

PEARLY GATES NATURAL FOODS INC.
2308 Memorial Parkway 8 West, 35801 • (205) 534-6233
M-Sat. 10-6:30

 On Memorial Pkwy. (Hwy 231), south of
Hwy 72, on the west side.

MOBILE
ORGANIC FOODS INC.
444B Azalea Road, 36609 • (205) 342-9554
M-Sat. 10-6

From I-65, take Airport Blvd. west. Turn left
on Azalea Rd. Store's 1 mile up on right.

TUSCALOOSA
MANNA GROCERY NATURAL GOURMET & ETHNIC FOODS
2312 McFarland Boulevard East, 35405 • (205) 752-9955
M-Sat. 9-7

From I-20/59, take McFarland Blvd. exit. From north: turn right.
From south: turn right, bear left on McFarland. Store's in
Meadowbrook Shopping Center.

ARIZONA

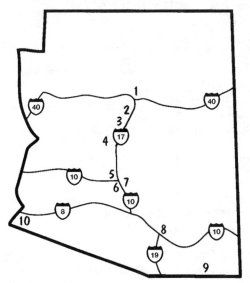

1. FLAGSTAFF
2. SEDONA
3. COTTONWOOD
4. PRESCOTT
5. PHOENIX
6. SCOTTSDALE
7. TEMPE
8. TUCSON
9. BISBEE
10. YUMA

BISBEE
BISBEE FOOD CO-OP
22 Main Street/Drawer DF, 85603 • (602) 432-4011
M-Sat. 9-6, Sun. 11-5

On Main St. in historic section, parallel to Rte. 80.
"Small town, hard to get lost."

COTTONWOOD
MOUNT HOPE NATURAL FOODS
1123 North Main Street, 86326 • (602) 634-8251
*One of the oldest natural food stores in Arizona, opened by Herb,
who grew up on Mt. Hope St. in New York and "wanted to bring a
little bit of the Bronx to Arizona." Homesick travelers, take note.*
M-Sat. 9-6, Sun. 10-5

From I-17, take Camp Verde/Cottonwood exit. Follow signs to
Cottonwood. Turn left on Main St., store's 3 miles up on the right.

Arizona ————————————————————

FLAGSTAFF
NEW FRONTIERS
801 South Milton (I-17), 86001 • (602) 774-5747
M-Sat. 9-8, Sun. 10-6

From I-40, take I-17 exit. Store's one mile south of I-40 on the left.

PHOENIX
REAY'S RANCH MARKET
4812 North 40th Street, 85018 • (602) 954-0584
Sun.-Sun. 8am-10pm

From I-17, take Camelback Exit. Head east about 10 miles.
Store's on right, on corner of Camelback and 40th St.

PRESCOTT
PRESCOTT NATURAL FOODS
330 West Gurley Street, 86301 • (602) 778-5875
M-F 9-7, Sat. 9-6, Sun. 12-5

Hwy 69 more or less becomes Gurley. Store's
on east side, one block past town square.

SCOTTSDALE
REAY'S RANCH MARKET
9689 North Hayden Road, 85258 • (602) 596-9496
Sun.-Sun. 7am-10pm

From I-10, take Rte. 202 north/east, then take 44th St. north (becomes
McDonald). Turn left on Hayden. Store's on right, in Mountain View Plaza.

SEDONA
NEW FRONTIERS
2055 West Highway 89A, 86336 • (602) 282-6311
M-Sat. 9-8. Sun. 10-8

On the east side of Hwy 89A in West Sedona. Not in the tourist section.

TEMPE
GENTLE STRENGTH CO-OP
234 West University, 85281 • (602) 968-4831
*Whenever I asked stores about other sources of organic food,
they all recommended this co-op.*
M-F 9-9, Sat. & Sun. 9-8

I-10/17, from west: turn left off University exit. You'll curve around alot.
Store's just past railroad tracks. From east: turn right off Broadway exit,
left on Mill Ave., and left on University. Store's on the right.

TUCSON
FOOD CONSPIRACY CO-OP
412 North 4th Avenue, 85705 • (602) 624-4821
M-Sat. 9-7:30, Sun. 10-6

From I-10, take St. Mary's exit east (becomes 6th St.). Turn right on
4th Ave. Store's on left.

REAY'S RANCH MARKET
3360 Speedway, 85716 • (602) 795-9844
Sun.-Sun. 7am-10pm

From I-10, take Speedway exit east about 6 miles. Store's on right, past
the University.

REAY'S RANCH MARKET
4751 East Sunrise, 85718 • (602) 299-8858
Sun.-Sun. 7am-10pm

From I-10, take Ina Rd. exit (becomes Sunrise) north/east. Store's on right.

— *LISTINGS* —

YUMA
YUMA HEALTH FOOD STORE
2099 South 4 Avenue, 85364 • (602) 783-5158

ARKANSAS

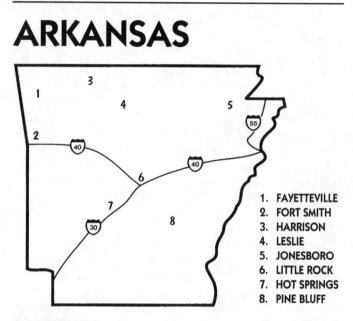

1. FAYETTEVILLE
2. FORT SMITH
3. HARRISON
4. LESLIE
5. JONESBORO
6. LITTLE ROCK
7. HOT SPRINGS
8. PINE BLUFF

FAYETTEVILLE
Ozark Natural Foods Co-op
213 West Dixon, 72701 • (501) 521-7558
M-F 10-6:30, Sat. 9-6:30, Sun. 1-5

From Rte. 71, turn west on
Dixon. Store's on left.

FORT SMITH
Olde Fashioned Foods
123 North 18th Street, 72901 • (501) 782-6183
M-Sat. 9-6

From I-40, take Rogers Ave exit and go south/ west
on Rogers Ave. Turn right on 18th Street. Store's in
yellow house on the left.

HARRISON
Almond Tree Inc.
126 North Willow Street, 72601 • (501) 741-8980
Small, mostly seasonal produce section.
M-F 9-5:30, Sat. 9:30-3

In the downtown square 1.5 blocks west
of Hwy 65. Take the Business 65 exit.

LESLIE
COVE CREEK CO-OP
Main Street, 72645 • (501) 447-2724
Limited produce, a large selection of pottery, and an organic bakery next door!
M,W, Th, F 9-5, Sat. 10-2

From Hwy 65, go east on Oak. Turn left on Main St. Store's on left.

LITTLE ROCK
BEANS & GRAINS & THINGS
300 South Rodney Parham, 72205 • (501) 221-2331
M-Sat. 8:30-7, Sun. 10-6

Off I-630, take Mississippi/Rodney Parham exit. Head north on Rodney Parham Rd. Store's on left, before road crosses Markham.

— *LISTINGS* —

HOT SPRINGS
OLD COUNTRY STORE
455 Broadway, 71901 • (501) 624-1172
Organic produce limited, but expanding!

JONESBORO
JONESBORO HEALTH FOODS
1321A Stone Street, 72401 • (501) 932-5301
No produce.

PINE BLUFF
SWEET CLOVER HEALTH FOODS
2624 West 28th Street, Old Village Shopping Center, 71603
(501) 536-0107
No produce.

NORTHERN CALIFORNIA

1. ARCATA
2. EUREKA
3. CHICO
4. MENDOCINO
5. UKIAH
6. COTATI
7. SONOMA
8. NAPA
9. DAVIS
10. SACRAMENTO
11. GRASS VALLEY
12. TRUCKEE
13. OLYMPIC VALLEY
14. TAHOE CITY
15. S. LAKE TAHOE
16. MARIN COUNTY
17. SAN FRANCISCO
18. BERKELEY
19. PACIFICA
20. HALF MOON BAY
21. BURLINGAME
22. PALO ALTO
23. JACKSON

ARCATA
ARCATA FOOD CO-OP
811 "I" Street, 95521 • (707) 822-5947
M-Sat. 9-9, Sun. 9-8

From US 101, take Samoa Blvd. exit west. Turn right on "I" St. Store's on left.

BERKELEY
ELMWOOD NATURAL FOODS
2944 College Avenue, 94705 • (510) 841-3871
M-Sat. 10-6, Sun. 12-5

From I-80, take Rte. 13 exit (Ashby Ave.). Turn left on College. Store's right there.

8

BERKELEY (cont.)

LIVING FOODS
1581 University Avenue, 94703 • (510) 549-1714
Sun.-Sun. 9am-8pm

From I-80, take University exit. Go about 2 miles east on University.
Store's on left.

MACROBIOTIC GROCERY & ORGANIC CAFÉ
1050 40th Street, 94608 • (510) 653-6510
M-F 7am-8:30pm, Sat. & Sun. 8am-8:30pm

From I-80, take 27th St. exit north. Turn left on Telegraph and left on
40th. Store's on right.

WHOLE FOODS MARKET
3000 Telegraph Avenue, 94705 • (510) 649-1333
Sun.-Sun. 9am-10pm

From I-80, take Ashby exit (Hwy 13). Store's on corner of Ashby and
Telegraph. Ave.

BURLINGAME

EARTHBEAM
1399 Broadway, 94010 • (415) 347-2058
M-Sat. 9-7, Sun. 10-6

 From I-101, take Broadway exit west.
Store's on left.

CHICO

CHICO NATURAL FOODS (CO-OP)
818 Main Street, 95928 • (916) 891-1713
M-Sat. 9-8, Sun. 10-5

From Hwy 99, take Hwy 32 exit. Head west on Hwy 32, (8th St.).
Store's on left, corner of 8th and Main St.

CORTE MADERA
SUPERNATURAL FOODS
147 Town Center, 94925 • (415) 924-7777
M-Sat. 9-8, Sun. 10-6

I-101, from south: store's right there, on left. From north: store's right off Tamalpais exit in Town Center Shopping Ctr.

COTATI
COTATI NATURAL FOODS CO-OP
8250 Old Redwood Hwy, 94928 • (707) 795-2790
M-F 9-8, Sat. & Sun. 9-7

From Hwy 101, take Cotati exit. Follow signs to town. Turn right onto Old Redwood Hwy. Store's on left.

DAVIS
DAVIS FOOD CO-OP
620 G Street, 95616 • (916) 758-2667
Sun.-Sun. 9am-10pm

From I-80, take Davis exit north (you'll be on E Street). Turn right on 6th. Store's on right, corner of 6th and G.

EUREKA
EUREKA CO-OP
333 First Street, 95501 • (707) 443-6027
M-Sat. 10-7, Sun.10-6

From Hwy 101 (which becomes 5th St. in town), turn left on E Street. Store's on left, corner of 1st and E St.

GRASS VALLEY
BRIAR PATCH COMMUNTIY MARKET (CO-OP)
10061 Joerschke Drive, 95945 • (916) 272-5333
M-Sat. 9-9, Sun. 10-5

From I-80, take Rte. 49 north to Grass Valley. Take Brunswick exit and turn left, turn left on Maltman, and right on Joerschke Dr. Store's on left.

HALF MOON BAY
HEALING MOON
523 Main Street, 94019 • (415) 726-7881
M-Sat. 10-6, Sun. 11-5

From Hwy 1, turn east on Kelley. Store's on left, corner of Kelley & Main.

JACKSON
GOLD TRAIL
625 South Highway 49, 95642 • (209) 223-1896
M-F 10-6, Sat. 10-5

 Store's on east side of Hwy 49.

MENDOCINO
CORNERS OF THE MOUTH
PO Box 367, 95460 • (707) 937-5345
Sun.- Sun. 9-7

 From Hwy. 1, take Main St. exit. Go west on Main, right on Lansing, left on Ukiah. Store's on left in a red church.

MILL VALLEY
WHOLE FOODS
414 Miller Avenue, 94941 • (415) 381-1200
Sun.-Sun. 9am-8pm

From I-101, take Tiburon Belvedere exit. Go west on East Blithedale, left on Camino Alto, and right on Miller Ave. Store's on left.

NAPA
THE GOLDEN CARROT
1621 West Imola Avenue, 94559 • (707) 224-3117
M-F 10-6, Sat. 10-5, Sun. 10-4

From Hwy 29, take Imola exit east. Store's in River Park Shopping Center on right.

California

OLYMPIC VALLEY
Squaw Valley Community Market
1600 Squaw Valley Road, 96146 • (916) 581-2014
M-Sat. 8-7, Sun. 9-7

From I-80, take Hwy 89 south,
and turn west on Squaw Valley Rd.
Store's on right, next to post office.

PALO ALTO
Whole Foods
774 Emerson, 94301 • (415) 326-8676
Sun.-Sun. 8am-10pm

From I-101, take University exit west and turn left on Emerson. Store's on right.

Country Sun
440 California Avenue, 94306 • (415) 324-9190
They've just opened Eco-Threads next door.
All organic and naturally dyed clothes!
Sun.-Sun. 9-9

From I-101, take Oregon Expressway west, turn right on El Camino
Real and right on California. Store's on left.

PACIFICA
Good Health Natural Foods
80 West Manor Drive, 94044 • (415) 355-5936
M-Th 9:30-8, F 9:30-7, Sat. 9:30-6, Sun. 12-6

From Hwy 1, take Manor Drive exit and head towards
ocean on Manor Dr. (soon after exit). Store's on left.

SACRAMENTO
Sacramento Natural Foods Co-op
1900 Alhambra Boulevard, 95816 • (916) 455-2667
Sun.-Sun. 9am-10pm

From any highway, take exit with closest letter to "S," and find S and
30th St. Alhambra is next to 30th St.

SACRAMENTO (cont.)
CARMICHAEL NATURAL FOODS
7630 Fair Oaks Boulevard, 95608 • (916) 944-7000
M-Th 9-7, F 9-4, Sun. 10-5 (closed Sat.)

From I-80, take Madison East exit and turn right (south) on Manzanita and left on Fair Oaks. Store's on right.

SAN ANSELMO
LIVING FOODS
222 Greenfield Avenue, 94960 • (415) 258-0660
Sibling of Berkeley Living Foods.
M-Sat. 9-8, Sun. 10-7

From I-101, take Central San Rafael Exit. From south: turn left on 3rd St. (becomes Red Hill Ave.), turn left on Sequoia, right on Greenfield Ave. Store's on left. From north: turn right on 3rd. Same as above.

SAN FRANCISCO
BUFFALO WHOLE FOOD & GRAIN CO.
1058 Hyde, 94109 • (415) 474-3053
Rob owns the two Buffalo stores, and he's really cool.
M-Sat. 9-9, Sun. 10-8

I-101, from north: take Lombard exit onto Van Ness, turn left on Clay Street, right on Hyde Street, store's on left. From south: take 9th Street exit north. 9th Street becomes Larkin. Turn right on California, right on Hyde Street. Store on left.

BUFFALO WHOLE FOOD AND GRAIN CO.
598 Castro Street, 94114 • (415) 626-7038
M-Sat. 9-9, Sun. 10-8

I-101, from south: follow signs to Golden Gate Bridge. Take Fell Street exit. Turn left on Divisadero (becomes Castro). Store's on right. From north: Lombard Street exit to Van Ness. Turn right on Fell, left on Divisadero. Store's on right.

California

SAN FRANCISCO (cont.)

GOOD LIFE GROCERY
448 Cortland Avenue, 94110 • (415) 648-3221
M-Sat. 9-8, Sun. 10-6

I-101, from north: take Army exit to Bayshore Blvd., Turn right on Cortland. Store's on left. From south: turn left off Silver Ave. exit. Turn left on Cortland. Store on left.

GOOD LIFE GROCERY
1524 20th Street 94107 • (415) 282-9204
M-Sat. 9-7:30, Sun. 10-6

I-101, From south: Take Vermont St. exit. Turn right on Vermont, left on 20th St. Store's on left. From north: Head south on Van Ness, turn left on 17th St., right on Connecticut St., left on 20th St. Store's on left.

INNER SUNSET COMMUNITY FOOD STORE
1319 20th Avenue, 94122 • (415) 664-5363
Sun.-Sun. 9:30am-8:30pm

 From I-280, take 19th Ave. exit (one way). Turn left on Irving, and right on 20th Ave. Store's on left.

THE NATURE STOP
1336 Grant Avenue, 94133 • (415) 398-3810
M-F 9am-10pm, Sat.-Sun. 10-9

I-101, from north: take Fremont exit west, turn right on 3rd (becomes Kerny, then Columbia) and right on Grant. Store's on right. From south: take last San Francisco exit before Bay Bridge. Turn left on 3rd. Same as above.

RAINBOW MARKET
1899 Mission Street (at 15th St.), 94103 • (415) 863-0620
M-Sat. 9-8:30. Sun. 10-8:30

From I-280 going north: take Civic Center/ San Francisco 101 exit, then take 101 North (Golden Gate Bridge/ Civic Center) exit (left). Take Mission St./Van Ness Ave. exit and turn left on Mission. Turn left on 14th, right on Minna and right on 15th to park.

SAN FRANCISCO (cont.)

REAL FOOD CO.
3939 24th Street, 94116 • (415) 282-9500
Sun.-Sun. 9-8

Store's in Noe Valley. Directions are close to Valencia Whole Foods. 24th Street is west of 21st Street. Cross streets are Noe and Sanchez.

REAL FOOD CO.
2140 Polk, 94109 • (415) 673-7420
Real Food Co. has two floors. The 2nd floor is not wheelchair accessible. Real Food Deli is two doors down.
Sun.-Sun. 9-9

Store's between Broadway and Vallejo.

REAL FOOD CO.
1234 Sutter, 94109 • (415) 474-8488
M-F 10-9, Sat. & Sun. 10-8

Store's on the east side of Van Ness (I-101 becomes Van Ness in the city).

REAL FOOD CO.
1023 Stanyon, 94117 • (415) 564-2800
Store is next door to Real Food Deli.
Sun.-Sun. 9-8

Store's up the hill from Golden Gate Park, in the Haight/Ashbury area. The cross street is Parnassas.

VALENCIA WHOLE FOODS
999 Valencia, 94110 • (415) 285-0231
Sun. -Sun. 9-9

From south on I-280, take San José exit (becomes Guerrero St.), turn right on 21st St., store's on corner of 21st and Valencia. From north on I-101, take Lombard St. exit and turn right on Van Ness, right on Mission, right on 21st. Same as above.

SAN RAFAEL
REAL FOOD CO.
770 West Francisco Boulevard, 94901 • (415) 459-8966
M-F 10-7, Sat. 10-6, Sun. 11-6

I-101, from south: take Francisco Blvd. exit, and turn right on West Francisco, store's on left. From north: take Anderson Dr. exit and merge right into Anderson. Fork left on to Francisco Blvd., store's on left.

California

SONOMA
Down to Earth Natural Market, Café & Deli
201 West Napa, 95476 • (707) 996-9898
Sun.-Sun. 8-8

From Rte. 12 (Napa St.), go south on 2nd St. Store's in The Marketplace.

SOUTH LAKE TAHOE
Grassroots
2040 Dunlap Drive, 96150 • (916) 541-7788
Sun.-Sun. 10-6 (Summer: 9:30-7)

Store's at int. of
Hwy 50 and 89.

TAHOE CITY
Tahoe Community Market
505 West Lake Boulevard, 96145 • (916) 583-3156
M-Sat. 9:30-6:30, Sun. 10-6

Deli Open Summer Only

From I-80, take Rte. 89 south to Tahoe City. Turn right on W. Lake
Blvd. Store's on right.

TRUCKEE
Truckee Community Whole Foods
11357C Donner Pass Road, 96161 • (916) 587-7426
M-Sat. 9-7, Sun. 10-6

From I-80, take Squaw Valley/Hwy 89 exit. From west: turn left off
ramp, take 1st left into Donner Plaza. From east: turn right off ramp,
take 1st left into Donner Plaza.

UKIAH
Ukiah Co-op
308B East Perkins, 95482 • (707) 462-4778
M-F 9-7, Sat. 10-6

From Hwy 101, take Perkins exit and
head west on Perkins. Store's on right.

SOUTHERN CALIFORNIA

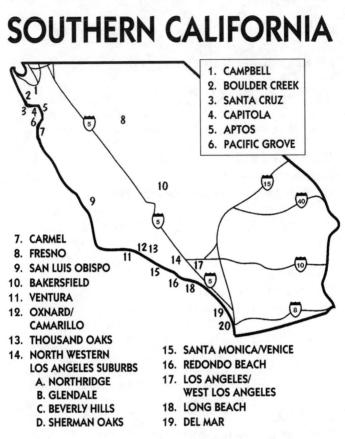

1. CAMPBELL
2. BOULDER CREEK
3. SANTA CRUZ
4. CAPITOLA
5. APTOS
6. PACIFIC GROVE

7. CARMEL
8. FRESNO
9. SAN LUIS OBISPO
10. BAKERSFIELD
11. VENTURA
12. OXNARD/
    CAMARILLO
13. THOUSAND OAKS
14. NORTH WESTERN
    LOS ANGELES SUBURBS
    A. NORTHRIDGE
    B. GLENDALE
    C. BEVERLY HILLS
    D. SHERMAN OAKS

15. SANTA MONICA/VENICE
16. REDONDO BEACH
17. LOS ANGELES/
    WEST LOS ANGELES
18. LONG BEACH
19. DEL MAR

APTOS

APTOS NATURAL FOODS
7506 Soquel Drive, 95003 • (408) 685-3334
Sun.-Sun. 9-8

From Rte. 1, take Seacliff Beach exit north. Turn left on Soquel. Store's on left in Aptos Shopping Center.

BAKERSFIELD

CONE'S HEALTH FOODS
2701 Ming Avenue, 93304 • (805) 832-5669
Mostly seasonal produce.
M-F 10-9, Sat. 10-7, Sun. 11-6

From Fwy 99: take Ming Ave. exit.
From north: stay in left lane going off ramp.
From south: "you'll be dumped right into parking lot."

17

BEVERLY HILLS
Mrs. Gooch's
239 North Crescent Drive, 90210 • (310) 274-3360
Sun.-Sun. 9-9

 From I-405, take
Santa Monica Blvd. exit east. Turn right on Crescent. Store's on right.

BOULDER CREEK
True Nature Foods
13070 Highway 9, 95006 • (408) 338-2105
M-Sat. 9-7, Sun. 10-6

 Store's on east
side of Hwy 9.

CAMARILLO
Lassen's Health Foods
2207 Pickwick Drive, 93010 • (805) 482-3287
M-Sat. 9-6:30

 I-101, from south: take Lewis Rd. exit, turn
left on Daily Drive, right on Arneill Rd.,
and left on Pickwick. From north: take Carmen Rd. exit, turn left on
Ventura Blvd., left on Arneill Rd., left on Pickwick. Store's on right.

CAMPBELL
Bread of Life Alternative Food Store
1690 South Bascom Avenue, 95008 • (408) 371-5000
Sun.- Sun. 8:30am-9pm

Off Hwy 17, take Hamilton Ave. exit. Turn east at first stoplight.
Store's on the left, corner of Hamilton and Bascom.

Sunflower Natural Foods
2230 South Bascom Avenue, 95008 • (408) 371-7800
M-Sat. 9-6:30, Sun. 11-6

From Hwy 17, head east on Hamilton and turn right on Bascom.
Store's on left.

CAPITOLA
NEW LEAF COMMUNITY MARKET
1210 41st Avenue, 95010 • (408) 479-7113
Sun.-Sun. 6:30-9

From Hwy 1, take 41st Ave. exit west. Store's on left, in Begonia Plaza.

CARMEL
CORNUCOPIA
26135 Carmel Rancho Blvd., Suite 557, 93923 • (408) 625-1454
M-Sat. 9-7, Sun. 10-6

From Hwy 1, take Carmel Valley Rd. east. Turn south on Carmel Ranch Blvd. Store's on left in Carmel Rancho Shopping Ctr.

DEL MAR
JIMBO'S NATURALLY
12853 El Camino Real Boulevard, 92130 • (619) 793-7755
Sun.-Sun. 9-9

From I-5, take Del Mar Heights exit east. Turn right on Camino Real. Store's on right in Del Mar Highlands Town Center on left.

FRESNO
CHRISTINA'S
761 East Barstow, 93710 • (209) 224-2222
M-F 9-7, Sat 9-6

From Rte. 41, take Shaw Ave. exit two blocks east. Turn left on 1st and left into Headline Shopping Center

GLENDALE
MRS. GOOCH'S
826 North Glendale, 91206 • (818) 240-9350
Sun.-Sun. 9-9

From Rte. 134, take Glendale Ave. exit north. Store's on right.

California

LONG BEACH
PAPA JON'S NATURAL FOODS
5006 East 2nd Street, 90803 • (310) 439-3444
Sun.-Th 8am-9pm, F & Sat. 8am-10pm

Follow I-710 to the end, turn right
on Ocean Blvd, left on Granada, and left on 2nd St. Store's on left.

LOS ANGELES
EREWHON NATURAL FOODS
7660 Beverly Boulevard, 90036 • (213) 937-0777
M-F 9-9, Sat. & Sun. 9-8

 Wine Only

From I-10 take Fairfax and Washington exit. Go north on Fairfax.
Turn right on Beverly. Store's on right.

NORTHRIDGE
MRS. GOOCH'S
9350 Reseda Boulevard, 91324 • (818) 701-5122
Sun.-Sun. 9-9

From Fwy 118, take Reseda Blvd.
exit south. Store's on left.

OXNARD
LASSEN'S HEALTH FOODS
3471 Saviors Road, 93033 • (805) 486-8266
M-Sat. 9:30-6:30

Fwy 101, from north: take Oxnard Blvd. exit
and head south. Oxnard becomes Saviors
(go south at "Five Points" and head for beach). Store's on the right.
From south: take Vineyard exit and turn left on Vineyard. Turn left on
Oxnard. Same as above.

PACIFIC GROVE
GRANARY MARKET
173 Central Avenue, 93950 • (408) 372-2533
Sun.-Sun. 9-8, (Winter: Sat. & Sun. 9-7)

From Hwy 1, take Del Monte Ave. west (becomes
Central in Pacific Grove). Store's on left.

REDONDO BEACH
Mrs. Gooch's
405 North Pacific Coast Highway, 90277 • (310) 376-6931
Sun.-Sun. 9-9

I-5, from north: turn right off Redondo Beach Blvd. exit, right on Artesia, left on Aviation Blvd. and left on Pacific Coast Hwy. Store's on left. From south: exit at Artesia Blvd. Same as above.

SAN DIEGO
Green Tree Grocer's
3560 Mt. Acadia Boulevard, 92111 • (619) 560-1975
M-Sat. 8am-9pm, Sun. 9-8

From I-805, take Balboa Ave. West exit one mile. Turn left on Genesee Ave., right on Mt. Alifan and right on Mt. Acadia. Store's .75 miles down on right.

Jimbo's Naturally
3918 30th Street, 92104 • (619) 294-8055
M-Sat. 9-8, Sun. 10-6

 From I-805, take University Ave. exit west and turn right on 30th St. Store's on left.

Ocean Beach People's Natural Foods Market
4765 Voltaire Street, 92107 • (619) 224-1387
M-F 9-9, Sat. & Sun. 9-8

Follow Hwy 8W as far as it goes. Turn left on Sunset Cliffs Blvd. and follow into Ocean Beach. Turn left on Voltaire St. Store's on right.

SAN LUIS OBISPO
Questa Co-op
745 Francis Street, 93401 • (805) 544-7928
Sun.-Sun. 10-7

From Hwy 101, take Marsh St. exit and go around the bend. Turn right on Broad St. Follow signs to airport. Turn left on Francis. Store's just behind Circle K Market, corner of Broad.

SANTA CRUZ
COMMUNITY FOODS
2724 Soquel Avenue, 95062 • (408) 462-0458
Sun.-Sun. 9am-8:30pm

 From I-1 (Hwy 1) Take Soquel Ave. exit and head north. Store's on left.

FOOD BIN HERB ROOM
1130 Mission Street, 95060 • (408) 423-5526
Sun.-Sun. 9-9

 Hwy 1 becomes Mission St. Store's on north side, on corner of Mission and Laurel.

NEW LEAF COMMUNITY MARKET
2351 Mission Street, 95060 • (408) 426-1306
Sun.-Sun. 9-9

New Leaf is farther north than Food Bin.

STAFF OF LIFE NATURAL FOODS MARKET
1305 Water Stret, 95062 • (408) 423-8632
Sun.-Sun. 9:30am-8:30pm

From Hwy. 1, take Morrissey exit south. Turn right on Water. Store's on right.

SANTA MONICA
CO-OPPORTUNITY CONSUMER CO-OP
1530 Broadway, 90404 • (310) 451-8902
Sun.-Sun. 9-9

 Off of I-10, turn left onto Broadway. Store's on left, corner of B'way and 16th St.

SHERMAN OAKS
MRS. GOOCH'S
12905 Riverside Drive, 91423 • (818) 762-5548
Sun.-Sun. 9-9

Off Fwy 101, go north one block off Coldwater Canyon exit. Store's on left.

THOUSAND OAKS
LASSEN'S HEALTH FOODS
2857 Thousand Oaks Boulevard, 91361 • (805) 495-2609
M-Sat. 9-8

From Fwy 101, take Hampshire St. exit. Go north on Hampshire, left on Thousand Oaks Blvd., right on Skyline Drive, and left into Skyline Plaza.

MRS. GOOCH'S
451 Avenida de los Arboles, 91360 • (805) 492-5340
Sun.-Sun. 9-9

From Fwy 101, take Filmore (Fwy 23) exit north. Turn left on Avenida de los Arboles. Store's on right.

VENICE
VENICE OCEAN PARK FOOD CO-OP
839 Lincoln Boulevard, 90291 • (310) 399-5623
Sun.-Sun. 9-9

From I-10, take Lincoln Blvd. Exit and head south, turn right on Brooks Ave., store's on right.

VENTURA
LASSEN'S HEALTH FOODS
4013 East Main Street, 93003 • (805) 644-6990
M-Sat. 9:30-6:30

Fwy 101, from south: take Telephone Road exit. Turn left on Telephone, right on Main, and right in PepBoys Plaza.
From north: take same exit on to Main. Same as above.

WEST LOS ANGELES
MRS. GOOCH'S
3476 Centinela Avenue, 90066 • (310) 391-5209
Sun.-Sun. 9-9

From I-10, take the Bundy South exit. Bundy becomes Centinela. Store's on left.

COLORADO

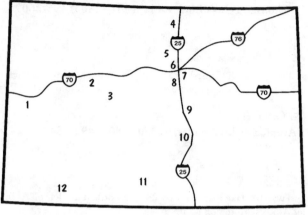

1. GRAND JUNCTION	5. BOULDER	9. COLORADO SPRINGS
2. GLENWOOD SPRINGS	6. DENVER	10. PUEBLO
3. ASPEN	7. AURORA	11. ALAMOSA
4. FORT COLLINS	8. LITTLETON	12. DURANGO

ALAMOSA
VALLEY FOOD CO-OP
7565 West Highway 160 #5, 81101 • (719) 589-5727
M-Sat. 9-6

 On Hwy 160, just west of Alamosa proper
in the Villa Mall.

ASPEN
SUNDAY'S TRUE FOOD CONNECTION
316B Aspen Airport Business Center, 81611 • (303) 925-5502
M-F 9-6, Sat. 10-6 (Extended hours in winter)

From Hwy 82, store's across from the airport (visible from road).

AURORA
WILD OATS
12131-F East Iliff Avenue, 80014 • (303) 695-8801
Sun.-Sun. 8am-10pm

 From I-225, turn west
on Iliff. Store's on
right, two miles down.

Colorado

BOULDER
ALFALFA'S
1651 Broadway, 80302 • (303) 442-0082
Sun.-Sun. 8am-10pm (Sun. 'til 9)

Take Arapahoe exit off I-36. Turn left on Arapahoe. Store's on left.

WILD OATS COMMUNITY MARKET
2584 Baseline Road, 80303 • (303) 499-7636
Sun.-Sun. 7am-11pm

From I-36, take Baseline Rd. exit west. Store's on left in Basemar Shopping Ctr.

COLORADO SPRINGS
MOUNTAIN MAMA NATURAL FOODS
1625 West Uintah, 80904 • (719) 633-4139
M-Sat. 9-7, Sun. 11-5

From I-25, take W. Uintah exit and head west about a mile. Store's on left.

WILD OATS MARKET
5075 North Academy, 80918 • (719) 548-1667
Sun.-Sun. 8am-10pm

From I-25 take Academy Exit, exit will lead to Academy. Turn east there. Store's in Union Square. Store's on left.

DENVER
WILD OATS MARKET
2260 East Colfax, 80206 • (303) 320-1664
Sun.-Sun. 8am-10pm

From I-70, take York St. exit south. Store's on right, corner of York and Colfax.

ALFALFA'S
900 East 11th Avenue, 80218 • (303) 832-7701
M-Sat. 7:30am-9:30pm, Sun. 8am-9pm

From I-25, take Spear Blvd. exit south. Turn left on 11th Ave. Store's on right.

Colorado

DURANGO
DURANGO NATURAL FOODS
575 East 8th Avenue, 81301 • (303) 247-8129
M-Sat. 8-8, Sun. 10-6

 Hwy 160, from east: turn north on Rte 3 (becomes 8th Ave.) Store's on left. From west: head north on Camino Del Ril, turn right onto 6th St. Store's on right, corner of 8th and 6th St. (College Dr.).

FORT COLLINS
ALFALFA'S
216 West Horsetooth Road, 80525 • (303) 225-1400
Sun.-Sun. 8am-9pm

From I-25, take Harmony Rd. exit, and head west (toward mountains). Go about 5 miles and turn right on College Ave. Turn left on Horsetooth. Store's on right.

FORT COLLINS CO-OP
250 East Mountain, 80524 • (303) 484-7448
"Fort Collins' original health food store!"
M-F 8:30-8, Sat. 8:30-7, Sun. 11-6

From I-25, take Mulberry exit west. Turn right on Remmington and right on Mountain. Store's on left.

WILD OATS
1611 South College Avenue 80525 • (303) 482-3200
M-F 8am-10pm, Sat-Sun. 8am-9pm

From I-25, take Prospect Rd. exit, head west on Prospect (toward mountains), just after College Ave., turn left into shopping center.

GLENWOOD SPRINGS
NATURALLY FOOD STORE
1001 Grand Avenue, 81601 • (303) 945-7180
M-Sat. 10-6

From I-70, take Glenwood Springs exit. Road that you're on becomes Grand Ave. Store's on right in Tamarack Sq.

GLENWOOD SPRINGS (cont.)
GOOD HEALTH GROCERY
730 Cooper Avenue, 81601 • (303) 945-0235
M-F 10-7, Sat. 10-5, Sun. 12-5

From I-70, take Glenwood Springs Exit. Turn left on 8th Ave.
Store's on right, at corner of Cooper.

GRAND JUNCTION
Sundrop Grocery
321 Rood Avenue, 81501 • (303) 243-1175
M-Sat. 9-6

I-70, from west take Fruita exit, from east take Airport exit.
Follow signs south to Grand Junction, heading down 7th St.
Turn right on Rood. Store's on left.

LITTLETON
ALFALFA'S
5910 South University Boulevard, 80121 • (303) 798-9699
Sun.-Sun. 8am-9pm

From I-25, take Hwy 285 west and left onto Rte. 85 (University).
Turn left on Orchard St. In the Cherry Hills Marketplace.

PUEBLO
AMBROSIA NATURAL FOODS & BUYER'S CO-OP
112 Colorado Avenue, 81001 • (719) 545-2958
M-F 10-7, Sat. 10-5

From I-25, take 1st St. exit. Head towards town on 1st St. Turn left
on Union, go over bridge and take right fork (Colorado Avenue).
Store's on left.

CONNECTICUT

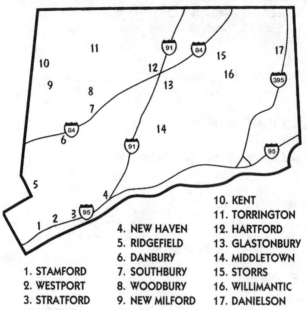

4. NEW HAVEN
5. RIDGEFIELD
6. DANBURY
7. SOUTHBURY
8. WOODBURY
9. NEW MILFORD

1. STAMFORD
2. WESTPORT
3. STRATFORD

10. KENT
11. TORRINGTON
12. HARTFORD
13. GLASTONBURY
14. MIDDLETOWN
15. STORRS
16. WILLIMANTIC
17. DANIELSON

DANBURY

CHAMOMILLE NATURAL FOODS
58-60 Newtown Road (Route 6), 06810 • (203) 792-8952
M-Sat. 9:30-6 (Th. 'til 8)

From I-84, take Exit #8 and follow road north/east for a half mile. Store's on right in Rte. 6 Plaza.

DANIELSON

COMMUNITY HEALTH FOODS
89 Main Street, 06239 • (203) 779-0033
M-W 8:30-5:30, Th. 8:30-6:30, Fri. 8:30-6, Sat. 9-5

From I-395, take Exit #92. Turn west on Westcott and left on Main. Store's on right.

GLASTONBURY
GARDEN OF LIGHT PURE FOODS MARKET
2858 Main Street, 06033 • (203) 657-9131
M-F 9:30-8, Sat. 9:30-5, Sun. 1-5

From I-91, take Putnam Bridge exit, cross bridge, take Main St. Glastonbury exit, turn left on Griswold and right on Main St. Store's on the left.

HARTFORD
CHEESE AND STUFF
550 Farmington Avenue, 06105 • (203) 233-8281
M-Sat. 8-8, Sun. 9-6

From I-84, take Sisson Ave. exit, turn right on Sisson Ave., left on Farmington Ave, and right on Kenyon. Store's on left, at corner.

KENT
KENKO NATURAL GROCERY
351 Kent Cornwall Road, 06757 • (203) 927-4079
Sun.-Sun. 9:30-7

On Rte. 7, about five miles north of Kent proper. Store's on west side.

MIDDLETOWN
IT'S ONLY NATURAL
686 Main Street, 06457 • (203) 346-1786
Dar's college town! Restaurant attached, great for holistic student dating.
M 9-5:30, Tu-Sat. 9-7, Sun. 11-4

From Rte. 9, take Exit #16 (left). At light after exit, turn left on Main St. Store's on left

NEW HAVEN
EDGE OF THE WOODS
379 Whalley Avenue, 06511 • (203) 787-1055
M-F 8:30-7:30, Sat. 'til 6, Sun. 9-6

From I-91, take Downtown exit. Exit street becomes Frontage St., turn right on Ella Grasso Blvd., right on Whalley Ave. Store's on left in Market Square Shopping Center.

NEW MILFORD
Bobbitt's Natural Foods
10 Bank Street, 06776 • (203) 355-1515
M-Sat. 9:30-5:30 (Th. 'til 7:30)

From I-84, take Exit #7, go north about 8 miles on Rte. 7 and 202. Take 202 into New Milford turn right over bridge into town, left onto and left across town green. It's the first store on right.

RIDGEFIELD
The Good Food Store
Copps Hill Commons, 06877 • (203) 438-7000
M-Sat. 10-6, Sun. 12-5

Store's on Rte. 35.

SOUTHBURY
Natural Merchant
142 Main Street North, 06488 • (203) 264-9954
Small restaurant attached, open 11-3.
Sun.-Sun. 9-6 (Th & F 'til 7)

From I-84 take exit #15 west. Store's less than a half mile down.

STAMFORD
Natural Nutrition
1055 High Ridge Road, 06905 • (203) 329-7400
M-F 9-7, Sat. 9-6, Sun. 11-5

From Merritt Pkwy (15), take Exit 35 and bear right. Store's a half mile out on left.

STORRS
BetterWays Marketplace
Route 195, 06268 • (203) 429-4517
Extensive, exclusively organic produce, and an all-vegetarian store.
M-Sat. 9:30-6

Store's on south side of Rte. 195, in Holiday Mall.

STRATFORD
NATURE'S WAY NATURAL FOODS
922 Barnum Avenue Cutoff, 06497 • (203) 377-3652
M-Sat. 9-9, Sun. 9-1

From I-95, take West Broad exit (#32). From east: turn left at first light, left on Main and right on Barnum. Store's on left. From west: turn left on Main. Same as above.

TORRINGTON
NATURAL LIFE
634 Migeon Avenue, 06790 • (203) 489-8277
M-Sat. 9-7

 Store's on Rte. 4, west of Rte. 8.

WESTPORT
FOOD FOR THOUGHT
221 Post Road, 06880 • (203) 226-5233
M-Sat. 8-7, Sun. 9-5

From I-95, take Exit 17. Turn left on Riverside Ave. and left on Sylvan Rd. Store's on right in West Bank Center.

WILLIMANTIC
WILLIMANTIC FOOD CO-OP
27 Meadow Street, 06226 • (203) 456-3611
M-F 9:30-8, Sat. 9-8, Sun. 10-5

From Rte. 44, go south on Rte. 32, which becomes Rte. 66, which becomes Main St. in Willimantic. Turn left on Walnut St. and right on Meadow. Store's on left.

WOODBURY
NEW MORNING COUNTRY STORE
15 Hollow Road, 06798 • (203) 263-4868
Coffee samples!
M-W, Sat. 9-6, Th. & F 9-7, Sun. 11-3:30

From I-84, take Exit 15. Take Rte. 6 north to Woodbury. Turn left on Hollow Rd. Store's on left.

DELAWARE

1. NEWARK
2. MILFORD
3. REHOBOTH BEACH

MILFORD
THE NATURE TRAIL INC.
915 North Dupont Highway, 19963 • (302) 422-0430
Plans to expand!
M, Tu, Th, F 10-6, Sat. 10-4, W 12-6

Store is on Hwy 113 (Dupont Hwy), on south-bound lane side, north of Milford.

NEWARK
NEWARK CO-OP
280 East Main Street, 19711 • (302) 368-5894
M-Sat. 10-8

Off I-95, take Rte. 896 exit and go north. Turn right on Delaware Ave., then left on Library Lane, then left on Main St. Store's on right.

REHOBOTH BEACH
PETER RABBIT HEALTH FOOD STORE
220 Rehoboth Avenue, 19971 • (302) 227-3177
Summer: Sun.-Sun. 9-7, Off-season: M-Sat. 10-6, Sun. 12-4

Off Hwy 1, take the bypass (1A). 1A is or becomes Rehoboth Ave., depending on how you approach it. Store's 2.5 blocks from ocean, across from fire station.

FLORIDA

1. PENSACOLA
2. TALLAHASSEE
3. GAINESVILLE
4. JACKSONVILLE
5. ST. AUGUSTINE
6. DAYTONA BEACH
7. ORLANDO
   A. ALTAMONTE SPR.
   B. CASSELBERRY
8. COCOA BEACH
9. HOBE SOUND
10. TEQUESTA
11. BOCA RATON
12. FT. LAUDERDALE
13. HOLLYWOOD
14. N. MIAMI BEACH
15. GREATER MIAMI
    A. MIAMI
    B. SOUTH MIAMI
    C. MIAMI LAKES
16. COCONUT GROVE
17. NAPLES
18. FORT MYERS/
    CAPE CORAL
19. SARASOTA
20. TAMPA
21. LARGO
22. CLEARWATER
23. PALM HARBOR

AVENTURA
(NORTH MIAMI BEACH)
UNICORN VILLAGE MARKET
3565 NE 207th Street, 33180 • (305) 933-1543
M-Th 8am-10:30pm, F-Sat. 8-11, Sun. 10am-10:30pm

At the Waterways Shops, just east of Biscayne (US1) and 207th St.

BOCA RATON
ALL AMERICAN NUTRITION, INC.
652 Glades Road, 33431 • (407) 395-9599
M-F 9-8:30, Sat. 9-6:30, Sun. 11-6

Store's 1 mile east of I-95 on Glades Rd. Store's on right in Oaks Plaza.

Florida

CAPE CORAL
BACK TO NATURE
1217 SE 47th Terrace, 33904 • (813) 549-7667
M-F 9-6, Sat. 9-5

From I-75, take Daniels Rd. exit, turn right on Hwy 41, left on College Pkwy. Go over bridge, turn right on Vincennes, and right on 47th. Store's on right, in a shopping strip.

CLEARWATER
NATURE'S FOOD PATCH
1408 Cleveland Street 34615 • (813) 443-6703
M-F 10-9, Sat. 'til 7, Sun. 12-6

From Hwy 19, turn west on Gulf-to-Bay, right on Highland and left on Cleveland. Store's on right.

COCOA BEACH
SUNSEED FOOD CO-OP INC.
275 West Cocoa Beach Causeway, 32931 • (407) 784-0930
Sun.-Sun. 10-6

From 520 Causeway, almost at the intersection of 520 and A1A, in the White Rose Shopping Ctr.

COCONUT GROVE
OAK FEED NATURAL FOODS
2911 Grand Avenue, 33133 • (305) 448-7595
M-Sat. 9am-10pm, Sun. 10am-9pm

From US1, head east on Virginia St., then turn left on Grand Ave. Store's on left.

DAYTONA BEACH
HARVEST HOUSE NATURAL FOODS
498 North Nova Road, 32114 • (904) 255-0780
M-Sat. 9-6. (W-Th 'til 7), Sun. 12-5

From I-95, take State Rd. 92 east, then turn left on Nova. Store's on left.

FORT LAUDERDALE
BREAD OF LIFE NATURAL FOOD MARKET & RESTAURANT
2388 North Federal Highway, 33305 • (305) 565-7423 (RICE)
Sun.-Sun. 9-9 (M 9-7, F & Sat. 'til 10)

 Wine Only

From I-95, take Oakland Park East exit east. Turn right on US1 (Federal Hwy). Store's on left.

ONLY NATURAL
3038 North Federal Highway, 33306 • (305) 563-4700
This store is near Bread of Life.

FORT MYERS
ADA'S NATURAL FOOD MARKET
3418 Fowler Street, 33901 • (813) 936-4756
M-Sat. 9-6

 From I-75, take Colonial exit (#22). Head west on Colonial. Turn right on Fowler. Store's on left.

GAINESVILLE
MOTHER EARTH MARKET
521 NW 13th Street, 32601 • (904) 378-5224
M-Sat. 9-9, Sun. 11-7

From I-75, take
Newberry Rd. exit (becomes University), and left 13th St. Store's on right.

HOBE SOUND
PEGGY'S NATURAL FOODS
9835 SE Federal Highway, 33455 • (407) 546-4458
M-F 9:30-6, Sat. 9:30-5

Store's on east side of Hwy 1 (Federal Hwy).

HOLLYWOOD
FOOD AND THOUGHT
3369 Sheridan Street, 33021 • (305) 961-1687
M-Sat. 9:30-7, Th 9:30-8, Sun. 11:30-5:30

 From I-95, take Sheridan St. exit, head west. Store's on right in Park Sheridan West Shopping Ctr.

Florida

JACKSONVILLE
THE GRANARY WHOLE FOODS, INC.
1738 Kingsley Avenue, 32073 • (904) 269-7222
M-Sat. 9-6

From I-295, take US17 exit, go south two miles on US17, right on
Kingsley. Get in left lane after train tracks, store's on left.

LARGO
PIONEER NATURAL FOODS
12788 Indian Rocks Road, 34644 • (813) 596-6600
Owner says they've got "the best hummus on the east coast."
M-F 9-6:30, Sat. 9:30-5

 From US19, take Rte 688 west. Turn
right on Indian Rocks Rd. Store's on left.

MIAMI
DIVINELY REAL FOODS
6901 Biscayne Boulevard, 33138 • (305) 757-6133
M-Sat. 10-8, Sun. 11-6

Biscayne Blvd is US1. Store's on east side, corner of US1 and 69th St.

ABUNDANT ENERGY SOURCES, INC.
14248 NW 7th Avenue, 33168 • (305) 685-0517
M-Th 9:30-5:30, F 9:30-6:30, Sat. 10-5

 From I-95, take 441 exit (#18).
Follow signs to 441 South (NW 7th)
and head south. Store's on the right, in Santa Fe Shopping Center.

NAPLES
SUNSPLASH MARKET
850 Neapolitan Way, 33940 • (813) 434-7221
M-Sat. 9-8, Sun. 10-6

From I-75, head west off Pine Ridge Rd. exit. Go south on US41 one
block and turn right on Neapolitan Way. Store's on left in Neapolitan
Way Shopping Center.

ORLANDO
CHAMBERLIN'S NATURAL FOODS
Winter Park Mall, 32792 • (407) 647-6661
There are four stores with the same hours and more or less the same stuff. See listings at the end of the state.
 M-Sat. 9-8:30 (F 'til 9), Sun. 11-5:30

From I-4, head east off Lee Rd. exit, take right on Orlando Ave., store's on left, across from mall.

PALM HARBOR
PALM HARBOR NATURAL FOODS INC.
US19 and Curlew, 34684 • (813) 786-1231
M-Sat. 9-7, Sun. 12-5

 At intersection of US19 and Curlew, in the Seabreeze Shopping Center.

PENSACOLA
EVER'MAN NATURAL FOODS (CO-OP)
1200 North 9th Avenue, 32501 • (904) 438-0402
M 8:30-8, T-Sat. 8:30-6:30

 From I-10, take I-110 south. Turn left off Cervantes exit and left on 9th. Store's on right.

SARASOTA
THE GRANARY (NORTH)
8421 North Tamiami Trail, 34243 • (813) 351-4671
M-Sat. 8:30am-9pm, Sun. 11-6

From I-75, take Exit #40 and head west on University Pkwy. Turn right on Tamiami Trail (US41). Store's on right.

THE GRANARY
1930 Stickney Point Road, 34231 • (813) 924-4754
M-Sat. 8:30am-9pm, Sun. 11-6

From I-75, take Clark Rd. exit (#37) west. Clark becomes Stickney after US41. Store's on left.

SARASOTA (cont.)

THE GRANARY
1451 Main Street, 34236 • (813) 366-7906
M-F 8:30-6:30, Sat. 8-6, Sun. 10-5

From I-75, take Fruitville Rd. exit (#39). Take Fruitville west, turn left on US301 and right on Mian St. Store's on right, four long blocks down, with a green awning.

SOUTH MIAMI

KOLIBRI FABULOUS NATURAL FOODS RESTAURANT & MARKET
6901 Red Road, 33143 • (305) 665-7447
M-Sat. 9-9, Sun. 10-7

From US1, head south on 57th St. (Red Rd.). Store's on left.

NATURAL FOOD MARKET
9455 South Dixie Highway, 33156 • (305) 666-3514
"More organic produce than anyone in the southeast!" Better check it out.
M-Sat. 9-9, Sun. 11-8

 On the east side of
South Dixie Hwy (US1)

ST. AUGUSTINE

DIANE'S NATURALFOOD MARKET
2085 State Road 3, 32084 • (904) 471-3796
No organic produce, though otherwise highly recommended by regional expert, Steve!
M-Sat. 9:30-8, Sun. 12-5

 From US1, turn east on Rte.
312, right on State Rd. 3 and
right into Portman Plaza.

TALLAHASSEE

NEW LEAF MARKET (CO-OP)
1235 Apalachee Parkway, 32301 • (904) 942-2557
M-Sat. 9-9, Sun. 12-6

From I-10, take US27 (Apalachee Pkwy) south (it takes a 90 degree turn at City Hall). Store's on right in Parkway Shopping Center

TAMPA
Nature's Harvest Market & Deli
1021 North MacDill Avenue 33607 • (813) 873-7428
M-F 9-9, Sat. 9-7, Sun. 11-6

From I-275, take Howard/Armenia exit. Take Armenia south, turn right on Cypress and right on MacDill. Store's on right.

Nature's Harvest Market & Deli
4802 Gunn Highway, 33624 • (813) 873-7428
Same hours as above and same stuff, but with beer and wine as well.
From I-275, take Busch Blvd. exit (#33). Go west on Busch (becomes Gunn). Store's on left.

TEQUESTA
Morning Sun Health Foods
120 Bridge Road, 33469 • (407) 747-0037
M-F 9:30-6, Sat. 9:30-5:30 (Deli open M-Sat. 11-3)

 From Hwy 1, turn west on Bridge Rd. (Bridge is one block south of Tequesta Dr.) Store's on left.

— LISTINGS —

ALTAMONTE SPRINGS
Chamberlin's Natural Foods
1086 Montgomery Road, 32714 • (407) 774-8866

CASSELBERRY
Chamberlin's Natural Foods
Lake Howell Sq., Rte. 436, 32707 • (407) 678-3100

MIAMI LAKES
Hale's Health Foods
16427 NW 67th Avenue, 33014 • (305) 821-5331

ORLANDO
Chamberlin's Natural Foods
7600 Dr. Phillips Blvd., 32819 • (407) 352-2130

Chamberlin's Natural Foods
Colonial Plaza, Colonial Dr., 32803 • (407) 894-8452

GEORGIA

1. MARIETTA
2. ATLANTA
3. ATHENS
4. AUGUSTA
5. SAVANNAH

ATHENS
PHOENIX NATURAL FOOD MARKET
Corner of Broad & Pulaski, 30601 • (706) 548-1780
M-Sat. 9:30-6

Broad St. is the main strip in Athens. Store is across the street from University of Georgia campus.

ZUCCINI'S
1055 Gaines School Road, 30605 • (706) 353-8066
M-Sat. 9-9, Sun. 12-9

Gaines School Road intersects with I-78. Store is in eastern part of Athens.

ATLANTA
RAINBOW GROCERY
2118 Decatur Road NE, 30033 • (404) 636-5553
M-Sat. 10-8, Sun. 11-5

From I-75, take I-85 north to Clairmont exit. Head south/east on Clairmont Rd. Store is .25 miles past VA Hospital on left in the North Decatur Plaza.

ATLANTA (cont.)

SEVANANDA
1111 Euclid Avenue, 30307 • (404) 681-2831
*The Southeast's largest & oldest natural foods cooperative. Little 5 Points is
the hip section of Atlanta. You can get anything pierced, just up the street!*
M-Sat. 10-9, Sun. 12-9

 From north: I-75 or I-85 South, take North Ave.
exit, turn left on North Ave, go 2 miles and turn
right on Moreland. Turn right on Euclid. Store's on left. From south: I-20, take
Moreland Ave. exit, turn left on Moreland, and left on Euclid. Store's on left.

AUGUSTA

FOODS FOR BETTER LIVING
2606 McDowell Street, 30904 • (706) 738-3215
No organic produce, but a nice store.
M-F 9-6, Sat. 9-5

From I-20, take Bobby Jones Expressway (520), turn left on
Wrightsboro Rd., left on Highland Ave. and right on McDowell.
Store's on right.

MARIETTA

LIFE GROCERY
1453 Roswell Road, 30062 • (404) 977-9583
M-Sat. 9-9, Sun. 11-8 (Winter Sun. 11-6)

From I-75, take Exit 112 (Roswell Rd.) west towards Kennesaw and
Marietta Square. Store's on right in New London Square.

SAVANNAH

BRIGHTER DAY NATURAL FOODS
1102 Bull Street, 31401 • (912) 236-4703
M-Sat. 10-6

From I-95, take I-16 exit, then turn right off Gwinett exit. Go right on
Whitaker St. and left on Park Ave. Store's on right (Look for mural of
organic tomatoes with sunglasses).

IDAHO

1. MOSCOW
2. BOISE
3. TWIN FALLS

BOISE

BOISE CONSUMER CO-OP
1674 Hill Road, 83702 • (208) 342-6652
M-Sat. 9-9, Sun. 10-7 (Winter, M-F 10-8, Sat. 9-8, Sun. 10-7)

From Rte. 84, take Broadway exit. Follow signs to hospital and get in right lane.
Turn right on Fort St. (becomes Harrison) and left on Hill Rd. Store's on right.

MOSCOW

MOSCOW FOOD CO-OP
310 West Third Street, 83843 • (208) 882-8537
Sun.- Sun. 9-7

From Rte. 95, turn west on Main St. Store is 2 blocks down on right.

TWIN FALLS

THE HEALTH FOOD PLACE
655 Blue Lakes Blvd., 83301 • (208) 733-1411
M-F 9:30-6, Sat. 10-5

From I-86, take Sun Valley/Wells, Nevada exit
(#173). Go into Twin Falls, cross Snake River and
the road turns into Blue Lakes Blvd. Store's on right in Centennial Square.

ILLINOIS

1. MT. CARROLL
2. DE KALB
3. PALATINE
4. EVANSTON
5. CHICAGO
6. NAPERVILLE
7. MATTESON
8. PEORIA
9. BLOOMINGTON
10. URBANA
11. SPRINGFIELD
12. MT. VERNON

BLOOMINGTON
COMMON GROUND GROCERY
516 North Main Street, 61701 • (309) 829-2621
M-Sat. 9:30-5:30

From Rte. 51, turn left on Market St. (both directions), go one block
and turn north on Main St. Store's on left.

CHICAGO
FOODWORKS
1002 West Diversey, 60614 • (312) 348-7800
M-F 9-8 (M & Th 'til 9), Sat. 8-8, Sun. 9-8

Store's 3 blocks west of Sherwyn's (see below), corner of Diversey
and Sheffield.

CHICAGO (cont.)
HEALTH WORKS
1244 West Belmont Avenue, 60657 • (312) 477-4800
M-F 8am-9pm, Sat. 8-7, Sun. 10-7

I-90/94, from north:take Kimball exit. Turn right on Kimball, left on Belmont. Store's on left. From south: take Belmont exit and head east. Store's on left.

NEW CITY MARKET
1810 North Halsted, 60614 • (312) 280-7600
M-F 9-9, Sat. & Sun. 9-7

From I-90/94, take North Ave. exit east and turn left on Halsted. Store's on left.

SHERWYN'S
645 West Diversey Parkway, 60614 • (312) 477-1934
All organic produce!
M-F 10-8, Sat.10-7, Sun. 11-6

From I-90/94, take California exit head east on Diversey for three miles. Store's on right.

WHOLE FOODS MARKET
1000 West North Avenue, 60622 • (312) 587-0648
Sun.-Sun. 8am-10pm

From I-90/94, take North Ave. exit. Go east on North, store's on corner of North & Sheffield (turn left on Sheffield). Store's north of I-290. There's also a North exit off I-55.

DE KALB
DUCK SOUP CO-OP
129 East Hillcrest, 60115 • (815) 756-7044
M,Tu, & F 10-7, W,Th 10-9, Sat.-Sun. 10-5

From I-88, take Annie Glidden exit and go north one mile. Turn left on 1st St., go one mile on 1st St. and turn right on Hillcrest. Store's on left.

EVANSTON
GREEN EARTH NATURAL FOODS
2545 Prairie Avenue, 60201 • (708) 864-8949
M-Sat. 10-6 (Th. 'til 7)

From I-94, take Old Orchard exit east, turn left on Crawford, right on Central St. and right on Prairie. Store's on left.

OAK ST. MARKET
1615 Oak Avenue, 60201 • (708) 864-0330
Sun.- Sun. 9-8

From I-94, take Dempster St. exit. Turn left on Oak. Store's on right.

NAPERVILLE
FRESH FIELDS
Iroquois Center, 1163 Ogden Ave., 60563 • (708)369-9800
M-Sat. 8am-9pm, Sun. 8-8

From I-88, take Naperville Rd. exit south. Turn right on Ogden. Store's on right.

NATURAL HEALTH FOODS, INC.
411 E. Ogden Avenue, 60563 • (708) 355-4840
M-F 9-6 (W 'til 7) Sat. 9-5

 Same as above! Corner of Ogden and Loomis.

PALATINE
FRESH FIELDS
1331 North Rand Road, 60067 • (708) 776-8080
M-Sat. 8am-9pm, Sun. 8-8

From I-53, take Rand exit west, and turn right into Park Place Shopping Center.

PEORIA
NATURALLY YOURS GROCERY & DELI
1301 Pioneer Parkway, 61615 • (309) 692-4448
No produce, but otherwise a good organic selection.
M-F 10:30-7, Sat. 10:30-5

From I-474, take Knoxville exit and head south and turn right on Pioneer Pkwy. Store's on right.

SPRINGFIELD
FOOD FANTASIES
1512 West Wabash, 62704 • (217) 793-8009
Carrots only.
M-F 9-8, Sat. 9-6, Sun. 1-5

 From I-55, take South Grand exit west (only goes one way). Turn left on MacArthur, which curves into Wabash. Store's on left.

URBANA
JERRY'S IGA
2010 South Philo Road, 61801 • (217) 367-1166.
Jerry's is a regular supermarket with a health food store inside.
Sun.-Sun. 24hrs From I-74, take Cunningham exit south. Cunningham becomes Vine. Turn left on Florida and right on Philo. Store's on left in Southgate Shopping Ctr.

— *LISTINGS* —

MT. CARROLL
STRADDLE CREEK FOOD CO-OP
112 West Market Street, 61053 • (815) 244-2667
No produce.

MT. VERNON
NATURE'S WAY FOOD CENTER
102 S. 4th South, 62864 • (618) 244-2327

MATTESON
SOUTH SUBURBAN FOOD CO-OP
21750 Main Street, 60443 • (708) 747-2256
A great members-only co-op. They honor other memberships and once-thru travelers.

INDIANA

1. MISHAWAKA
2. GOSHEN
3. FORT WAYNE
4. WEST LAFAYETTE
5. INDIANAPOLIS
6. ANDERSON
7. GREENFIELD
8. RICHMOND
9. BLOOMINGTON

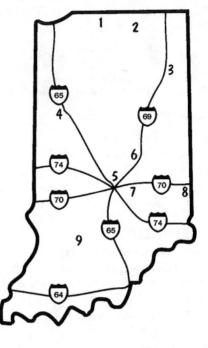

BLOOMINGTON

BLOOMINGFOODS (CO-OP)

3220 East Third, 47401 • (812) 336-5400

There are two stores. Third St.'s a little bigger, Kirkwood's a little groovier.

Sun.-Sun. 8am-10pm

Off Hwy 37, take the 46 Bypass. Go left on Third St., Store's on right.

BLOOMINGFOODS (CO-OP)

419 East Kirkwood Avenue, 47403 • (812)336-5300

Less seating, less parking, no alcohol & a 2nd floor (no wheechair access).

M-Sat. 8-8, Sun. 9-7

Off Hwy 37, take 46 Bypass. Turn right on College Ave., then left on Kirkwood Ave. Store's on left, down a little alley.

Indiana ─────────────────────────

FORT WAYNE
THREE RIVERS CO-OP NATURAL FOODS & DELI
1126 Broadway, 46802 • (219) 424-8812
M-F 9-8, Sat. 9-6, Sun. 12-6

Off I-69, take Take US 24 (becomes Jefferson Blvd.) east into Fort
Wayne. Turn right on Broadway. Store's on right.

GOSHEN
CENTRE-IN CO-OP
206 East Lincoln Avenue 46526 • (219) 534-2355
M-Sat. 9:30-6, Th. 'til 8

From Hwy 33, store's east on
Hwy 4 (Lincoln Ave.), on the right.

GREENFIELD
THE GOOD THINGS NATURALLY
610 Main Street, 46140 • (317) 462-2004
M, Tu,Th, F 10-6, Sat. 10-2 (closed W & Sun)

From I-70, take Rte. 9 south, turn right on
Rte. 40 (Main St.), Store's on right.

INDIANAPOLIS
GOOD EARTH NATURAL FOOD STORE
6350 North Guilford Avenue • (317) 253-3709
*It's in the Broad Ripple section: music, international restaurants,
a nearby park & a beautiful store in a 100 year-old house.*
M-Sat. 9-7, Sun. 12-5

From north side of the I-465 loop, go south on
US 31 about 3 miles. Turn left on 71st St. Turn
right on College Ave., then left on 64th St. Guilford is 3rd street on the right.

VINTAGE WHOLE FOODS
7391 North Shadeland Avenue, 46250 • (317) 842-1032
MWF 9-7, Tu & Th 9-8, Sat. 9-6, Sun. 12-5:30

I-465, from south: take Shadeland Ave. North exit.
Store's in the Shadeland Station Shopping Center
on right. From north: take Rte. 37 south. Go east on 75th. Store's on left.

MISHAWAKA
GARDEN PATCH MARKET
228 West Edison Road, 46545 • (219)255-3151
M-Sat. 10-7

 From Rte. 20, turn north on Grape Road, then right on Edison Rd. Store's on left.

RICHMOND
CLEAR CREEK FOOD CO-OP
Box E 487 Earlham College, 47374 • (219) 983-1547
Earlham is a renowned progressive Quaker College.
Summer: M-F 11-6, Sat. 11-5. School yr.: M-Th 10-8, F & Sat. 'til 7, Sun. 11-5

Deli during school year only

From I-70, take Williamsburg Pike south (towards Earlham College). Turn right on Hwy. 40, then left on College Ave. Turn right at "Earlham College D Street" entrance, and turn left at the end. In same building as maintenance and security.

WEST LAFAYETTE
GOODNESS GROCERY (CO-OP)
307 Sagamore Parkway West, Suite D, 47906 • (317) 463-3663
Sun.-Sun. 9-9

From I-65, take state road 25 towards Lafayette, turn right on US 52 (Sagamore Pkwy). Store's 3 miles north on the left in the K-Mart Plaza.

— *LISTINGS* —

ANDERSON
FRIST HEALTH FOOD CENTER, INC.
1203 East 53rd Street, 46013 • (317) 642-8992

With Dar's book and a bottle of hot sauce, we're ready to tour for all eternity!
- The Nields

IOWA

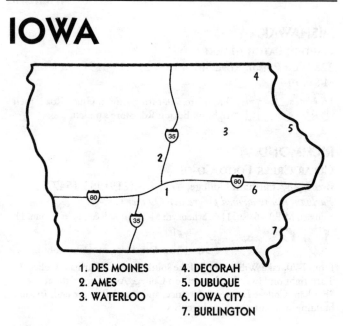

1. DES MOINES
2. AMES
3. WATERLOO

4. DECORAH
5. DUBUQUE
6. IOWA CITY
7. BURLINGTON

AMES

WHEATSFIELD FOOD CO-OP
413 Douglas Avenue North, 50010 • (515) 232-4094
M-Sat. 8am-9pm, Sun. 9-9

 From Rte. 35 take the 13th St. exit and go west about 3 miles. Turn left on Duff, right on 6th, and left on Douglas. Store's on right.

DECORAH

ONEOTA COMMUNITY FOOD CO-OP
521 West Water Street, 52101 • (319) 382-4666
M-Sat. 9-6 ('til 9 on Th), Sun. 12-4

From Hwy 52N, take Hwy 9 east, turn left on Short St. (becomes Mechanic), and left on Water St. Store's on left.

DES MOINES

NEW CITY MARKET
4721 University Avenue, 50311 • (515) 255-7380
M,W,F 10-6:30, Tu & Th 10-8, Sat. 9-6, Sun 11-5

I-235, from east: go north three blocks on 42nd, left on University. Store's on right.
From west: take 63rd north, left on University. Store's on left.

DUBUQUE
BREITBACH'S FARMERS' MARKET FOOD STORE
1109 Iowa Street, 52001 • (319) 557-1777
M-Th. 10-5:30, F & Sat. 8-5

 Just off Hwy. 61 at intersection of 61 & 151, in downtown area, near City Hall.

IOWA CITY
NEW PIONEER CO-OP
22 South Van Buren Street, 52240 • (319) 338-9441
Sun.-Sun. 8am-9pm

From I-80, take University of Iowa exit (#244). Go on Dubuque St. until it ends. Turn left on Washington St., store's on left.

WATERLOO
GREEN FIELDS HEALTH FOOD CENTER
2920 Falls Avenue, 50701 • (319) 235-9990
Very limited produce.
M-F 9-6, Sat. 9-5

From I-20, go north on Green Hill Rd. Turn left on University and left on Falls. Store's on left.

— *LISTINGS* —

BURLINGTON
NATURE'S CORNER
423 Jefferson Street, 52601 • (319) 754-8653
No produce.

KANSAS

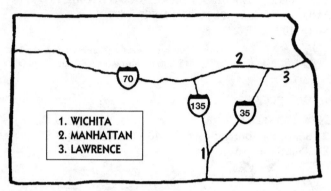

1. WICHITA
2. MANHATTAN
3. LAWRENCE

LAWRENCE
COMMUNITY MERCANTILE (CO-OP)
901 Mississippi Street, 66044 • (913) 843-8544
M-Sat. 8am-9pm, Sun. 10-9

From I-70 take East Lawrence exit. At stop sign turn left on N 2nd St. 2nd St. becomes Vermont after you cross bridge. Turn right on 9th. It's a big yellow building on the corner of 9th and Mississippi on left.

WILD OATS
1040 Vermont Street, 66044 • (913) 865-3737
Sun.-Sun. 7am-10pm (Winter 8-10)

Same directions as above, but don't turn on 9th St. Store's about two miles down on the left.

MANHATTAN
PEOPLE'S GROCERY (CO-OP)
811 Colorado, 66502 • (913) 539-4811
Tu-F 10-6, Sat. 9-5

 From I-70, take Manhattan/Hwy 177 exit about eight miles north. Hwy 177 becomes Pierre. Turn left on Juliette and right on Colorado. Store's on left.

WICHITA
FOOD FOR THOUGHT
2819 East Central Avenue, 67214 • (316) 683-6078
M-F 9:30-6, Sat. 9:30-5

I-135, from north, take Central Ave. exit and head east about ten blocks. Store's on right. From south take 1st St. exit, head east and turn left on Grove St. Turn right on Central. Store's on right.

NATURE'S MERCANTILE LTD.
2900 East Central Avenue, 67214 • (316) 685-3888
M-F 10-6, Sat. 9-5:30

From I-235, take Central Ave. exit east to Erie. Store's on corner of Erie and Central.

KENTUCKY

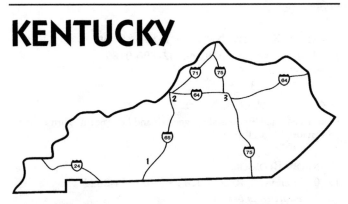

1. BOWLING GREEN   **2. LOUISVILLE**   **3. LEXINGTON**

BOWLING GREEN
WHOLE EARTH GROCERY
939 Broadway, 42101 • (502) 842-5809
M-F 10-6, Sat. 10-6, Sun. 12-6

From I-65, take Scottsville Rd exit and head north. Scottsville becomes Broadway. Store's on left.

Kentucky ─────────────────

LEXINGTON
GOOD FOODS CO-OP
439 Southland Drive, 40503 • (606) 278-1813
M-F 9:30-8, Sat. 9:30-7, Sun. 12-6

From I-64, take 922 south. At 4 circle, take Nicholasville Rd. towards and through town. Turn right on Southland. Store's on right.

LOUISVILLE
GOOD NEIGHBOR CO-OP GROCERY
2255 Frankford Avenue, 40202 • (502) 899-1991
M-F 10-8, Sat. 10-6, Sun. 12-5

From Hwy 71, head west on Zorn and turn left on Frankford. Store's on left.

RAINBOW BLOSSOM NATURAL FOODS STORE & DELI
106 Fairfax Avenue, 40207 • (502) 896-0189
M-Sat. 9-9, Sun. 12-6

From I-264, take Breckenridge Lane exit and head north. Turn right on Dayton, left on Fairfax. Store's on left.

RAINBOW BLOSSOM
12401 Shelbyville Road, 40243 • (502) 244-2022
Store's connected to bakery.
M-Sat. 9-9, Sun. 12-6

From I-265, take Hwy 60 exit towards town. Store's on right.

LOUISIANA

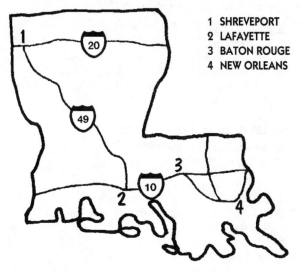

1 SHREVEPORT
2 LAFAYETTE
3 BATON ROUGE
4 NEW ORLEANS

BATON ROUGE
OUR DAILY BREAD MARKET & BAKERY
9414 Florida Blvd., 70815 • (504) 924-9910
M-Sat. 9-6, Sun. 12-5

From I-12, take Hwy 61 North exit towards Baton Rouge.
Turn right on Florida. Store's on right.

LAFAYETTE
OIL CENTER HEALTH FOODS
326 Travis, 70503 • (318) 232-7774
Little or no organic produce.
M-F 9:30-5, Sat. 9:30-4

From I-10, go east on Hwy 90, turn left on Ambassador, left on
College, left on Coolidge and left on Travis. Store's on right.

Louisiana

NEW ORLEANS
ALL NATURAL FOODS AND DELI
5517 Magazine Street, 70115 • (504) 891-2651
M-F 10-7, Sat. 9-7, Sun.10-5

From I-10, take Carrollton exit and head south/west towards river.
Turn left on St. Charles Ave., right on Nashville, and left on Magazine.
Store's on left.

EVE'S MARKET
7700 Cohn Street, 70118 • (504) 861-1626
M-Sat. 10-7, Sun. 11-5

From I-10, take Carrollton Ave. exit south. Cross Hwy 90 and turn left
on Cohn. Store's on right.

WHOLE FOODS MARKET
3135 Esplanade, 70119 • (504) 943-1626
Sun.-Sun. 9-9

I-10, from west: follow signs to New Orleans business district. Take
Metairie Rd./City Park exit and turn left on City Park. Turn left on
Carrollton and right on Esplanade. Store's on left. From east: go to I-
610. Take Paris Ave. exit and turn left at bottom of exit. Turn right on
Gentilly Blvd. and stay in middle lane. Turn right on Ponce De Leon.

SHREVEPORT
GOOD LIFE HEALTH FOODS & DELI
6132 Hearne Avenue, 71108 • (318) 635-4753
No organic produce, but they've tried many times and are very well-stocked!
M-F 9-5, Sat. 10-5

From I-20, take Hearne Ave. exit south. Store's on right, in a building
with other stores.

MAINE

1. BIDDEFORD
2. PORTLAND
3. DAMARISCOTTA
4. ROCKLAND
5. WATERVILLE
6. UNITY
7. BELFAST
8. BANGOR
9. BREWER
10. ORONO
11. ELLSWORTH

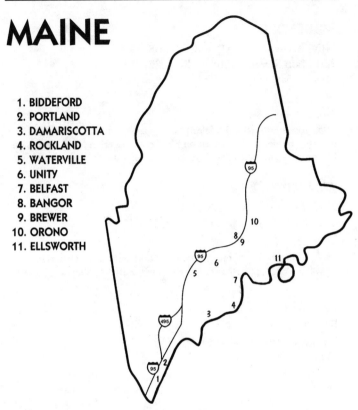

BANGOR

NATURAL LIVING CENTER
570 Stillwater Avenue, 04401 • (207) 990-2646
M-Sat. 9:30-7, Sun. 12-5

From I-95, take Bangor Mall exit. Store's just behind mall at cinema entrance.

BELFAST

BELFAST CO-OP
69 High Street, 04915 • (207) 338-2532
Winter: M-Sat. 9-6 (Summer: 8-7)

From Rte. 1, take north Belfast exit (of 2). Follow signs to hospital.
Store's on right, 1 mile past hospital.

BIDDEFORD
NEW MORNING NATURAL FOODS
230 Main Street, 04005 • (207) 282-1434
M-Sat. 9-5:30 (Th 'til 6) (The cafe is open M-F 11-3)

I-95, from south: take Biddeford exit (#4). Go left on Rte. 111 to "5 points in Biddeford." Turn left on Elm St. and right on Main. Store's on left. From north: take Exit #5 (Saco) south on Main St. Store's on right.

BREWER
NATURAL LIVING CENTER
421 Wilson Street, 04412 • (800) 933-4229
M-Sat. 9-6 (F 'til 6:30)

 From I-95, take N. Main St. exit. Turn right on Main. Store's on left in Brewer Shopping Center.

DAMARISCOTTA
RISING TIDE CO-OP
Business Route 1, 04543 • (207) 563-5556
M-Sat. 9-5:30 (Th 'til 7)

From Rte. 1, get on Business Rte. 1.
Store's 1.5-2 miles from Rte. 1 on west side.

ELLSWORTH
JOHN EDWARD'S WHOLE FOODS MARKET
165 Main Street, 04605 • (207) 667-9377
M-Th 9-5:30, F 9-6, Sat. 9-5

Rte. 1 is Main St. Store's on south/east side.

PORTLAND
GOOD DAY MARKET (CO-OP)
155 Brackett Street, 04102 • (207) 772-4937
M-F 10-8, Sat. 9-7, Sun. 11-7

From I-295, take Forest Ave. exit and head east. Get on to State St. (Rte. 77, one way), right on Pine St. and left on Brackett. Store's on left.

PORTLAND (cont.)
THE WHOLE GROCER
118 Congress, 04101 • (207) 774-7711
M-Sat. 9-8, Sun. 11-6

From I-295, take Franklin Arterial exit (one direction). Turn left on Congress. Store's on right.

ROCKLAND
GOOD TERN CO-OP
216 S. Main Street, 04841 • (207) 594-9286
M-F 9:30-6, Sat. 9:30-5

From Rte. 1, head south on Main St. It's trickier coming from north due to a short spell on a route that's parallel to Rte. 1. Store's on right.

UNITY
MAIN ST. MARKET (CO-OP)
PO Box 148, Route 202/9, 04988 • (207) 948-6161
M-F 9-6, Sat. 10-5

 A stone's throw from intersection of 202 and Rte. 139.

WATERVILLE
NEW MOON RISING NATURAL FOODS
110 Pleasant Street, 04901 • (207) 873-6244
Store just expanded. Big plans for 1994!
M-Sat. 9-6 (F 'til 7), Sun. 10-5

From I-95, take Main St. exit. Follow signs to Waterville. Store's on right.

— *LISTINGS* —

ORONO
THE STORE/AMPERSAND
22 Mill Street, 04473 • (207) 866-4110
No produce.

MARYLAND/D.C.

1. COCKEYSVILLE
2. TOWSON
3. PIKESVILLE
4. BALTIMORE
5. COLUMBIA
6. ANNAPOLIS
7. D.C. SUBURBS
   A. MT. RAINIER
   B. COLLEGE PARK
   C. SILVER SPRING
   D. BETHESDA
   E. CABIN JOHN

8. WASHINGTON D.C.
9. ROCKVILLE
10. FREDERICK

ANNAPOLIS

COUNTRY SUNSHINE MARKET
115 Annapolis Street, 21401 • (410) 268-6996
M-F 10-6, Sat. 10-5

From Hwy 50, take Rowe Blvd. exit toward downtown Annapolis. Get in left lane and turn left on Melvin and right on Annapolis. Store's on right.

FRESH FIELDS
2504 Solomon's Island Road, 21401 • (410) 573-1802
M-Sat. 8am-10pm, Sun. 8-8

Heading east on Hwy 50, take Aris T. Allen/Riva Rd. exit and follow signs to Solomon Island Rd. Turn left on Solomon Island Rd. Store's one mile down.

BALTIMORE

GOLDEN TEMPLE
2322 North Charles Street, 21218 • (410) 235-1014
M-F 9:30-7, Sat. 9:30-6, Sun. 11-5

From Baltimore Beltway (I-695), take I-83 exit south. Take 29th exit, turn right on Maryland, left on 23rd and left on Charles. Store's on left.

BETHESDA
FRESH FIELDS
5269 River Road, 20816 • (301) 984-4860
M-Sat. 8am-9pm, Sun. 8am-8pm

From I-495, take River Rd. South exit towards Wash. DC about 4 miles. Store's in Kenwood Station Shopping Center on left.

CABIN JOHN
BETHESDA CO-OP
6500 Seven Locks Road, 20818 • (301) 320-2530
M-Sat. 9-9, Sun. 9-7

From I-495 take River Rd. exit west (towards Potomac) and left on Seven Locks Rd.

Store's at MacArthur Blvd. in MacArthur Shopping Ctr.

COCKEYSVILLE
THE NATURAL
560 Cranbrook Road, 21030 • (410) 628-1262
M-F 9:30-8, Sat. 10-6, Sun. 11-6

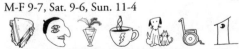

From I-83, take Padonia Rd. exit east, turn left on York and right on Cranbrook. Go .75 miles. Store's in Cranbrook Shopping Ctr. on left.

COLLEGE PARK
BEAUTIFUL DAY TRADING CO.
5010 Berwyn Road, 20740 • (301) 345-6655
M-Sat. 9-7:30, Sun. 10-4

From I-495, take Rte. 1 /Baltimore Ave. exit (#25) toward College Park about 1.5 miles. Turn left on Berwyn. Store's on left.

COLUMBIA
DAVID'S NATURAL MARKET
5430-C Lynx Lane, 21044 • (410) 730-2304
M-F 9-7, Sat. 9-6, Sun. 11-4

From Hwy 29, take Columbia Town Center (Rte. 175) exit west. Take Governor Warfield Pkwy right as the road forks. Turn right on Twin Rivers and left on Lynx. Store's on right in Village of Wild Lake Shopping Ctr.

Maryland/DC

DISTRICT OF COLUMBIA
AFTER THE HARVEST
1512 U Street NW, 20009 • (202) 234-6424
T-Sat. 10-8, Sun. 1-6

 From I-495, take NY Ave. exit. Turn right on Florida (becomes U). Store's on left.

HUGO'S NATURAL FOODS
3813-3817 Livingston Street NW, 20015 • (202) 966-6103
M-Sat. 9-8, Sun. 10-6

 Wine Only

From I-495, take Connecticut Ave. exit south. Store's on right, corner of Conn. & Livingston.

YES NATURAL GOURMET
1825 Columbia Road NW, 20009 • (202) 462-5150
M-Th 9-8, F & Sat. 9-7, Sun. 12-6

From I-495 loop, take Connecticut Ave. exit south, turn left on Calvert and right on Columbia. Store's on right.

YES NATURAL GOURMET
3425 Connecticut Avenue NW, 20008 • (202) 363-1559
M-Sat. 9-9, Sun. 10-8

Same directions as Hugo's, but Yes is a half mile further south, on the left, near the zoo (at the Cleveland Park metro stop).

FREDERICK
COMMON MARKET CO-OP
5813 Buckeystown Pike, 21701 • (301) 663-3416
M-Sat. 10-7, Sun. 12-5

From I-70, take Frederick/Buckeystown exit. Go south on Rte. 85 (Buckeystown Pike). Store's on left.

MT. RAINIER
GLUT FOOD CO-OP
4005 34th Street, 20712 • (301) 779-1978
Their motto: "Still cheap, still funky."
M-Sat. 10-7 (Th & F 'til 8), Sun. 10-5

   From Rte. 1 head west on 34th St. Store's on right.

PIKESVILLE
VILLAGE MARKET NATURAL GROCER
7006 Reisterstown Road, 21215 • (410) 486-0979
Expanding in 1994.
M-F 9:30-8, Sat. 9:30-6, Sun. 9:30-5

From I-695, take Hwy 140 (Reisterstown Rd.) exit (#20) south.
Store's 2 miles down on right, in Colonial Village Shopping Ctr.

ROCKVILLE
FRESH FIELDS
11503 Rockville Pike, 20852 • (301) 984-4880
M-Sat. 8-9, Sun. 8-8

From I-495, take North Rockville Pike exit (Rte. 355). Store's on right.

SILVER SPRING
TACOMA PARK & SILVER SPRINGS CO-OP
623 Slago Avenue, 20910 • (301) 588-6093
Sun.-Sun. 9-9

   From I-495 take Georgia Ave. exit. south and
turn left on Slago. Store's on left.

TOWSON
THE HEALTH CONCERN
28 West Susquehanna Avenue, 21204 • (410) 828-4015
M,W & Sat. 9:30-6, Tu,Th, & F 9:30-8, Sun. 12-5

From I-695, take Exit 26 south. Turn right on Washington. Go about
4 blocks and down a hill. Turn left on Susquehanna. Store's on left.

MASSACHUSETTS

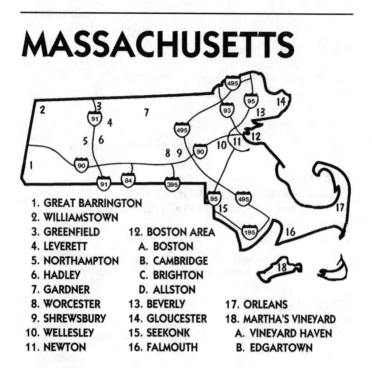

1. GREAT BARRINGTON
2. WILLIAMSTOWN
3. GREENFIELD
4. LEVERETT
5. NORTHAMPTON
6. HADLEY
7. GARDNER
8. WORCESTER
9. SHREWSBURY
10. WELLESLEY
11. NEWTON

12. BOSTON AREA
    A. BOSTON
    B. CAMBRIDGE
    C. BRIGHTON
    D. ALLSTON
13. BEVERLY
14. GLOUCESTER
15. SEEKONK
16. FALMOUTH

17. ORLEANS
18. MARTHA'S VINEYARD
    A. VINEYARD HAVEN
    B. EDGARTOWN

ALLSTON
Harvest Co-op Supermarket
449 Cambridge St., 02134 • (617) 787-1416
M-Sat. 9-10, Sun. 12-9

From I-90, take Allston exit, which puts
you on Cambridge. Store's on right.

BEVERLY
A New Leaf
261 Cabot St., 01915 • (508) 927-5955
M-Sat. 9:30-6:00 (Th 'til 8), Sun. 12-4

From I-95, get on to Rte.128 North. Turn right on Rte. 62 (Elliott St.)
and follow it to the end. Turn right on Cabot St. Store's on left.

BOSTON
Nature Food Center
545 Boyleston St., 02116 • (617) 536-1226
M-F 8-8, Sat. 9-7, Sun. 12-6

Store's in Copley Square, in the middle of the city,
less than a mile south of the Boston Common.

BRIGHTON
BREAD & CIRCUS
15 Washington St., 02146 • (617) 738-8187
M-Sat. 9-9, Sun. 12-8

From I-90 take Brighton/Allston exit and get on Cambridge St. (one direction) and turn left on Washington St. Store's on left.

CAMBRIDGE
BREAD & CIRCUS
115 Prospect Street, 02139 • (617) 492-0070
M-Sat. 9-9, Sun. 12-8

From I-90, take Cambridge exit, cross bridge and continue straight on River St. Cross Massachusetts Ave. River becomes Prospect. Store's on left.

CAMBRIDGE NATURAL FOODS
1670 Massachusetts Ave., 02138 • (617) 492-4452
M-Sat 9-8, Sun. 11-8

From Rte. 2 (coming from the west only), bear left on Alewife Brook Pkwy (Rte. 16 east) and turn right on Mass. Ave. Store's on right, about two miles down. Look for the big carrot on store sign.

HARVEST CO-OP SUPERMARKET
581 Mass. Ave., 02139 • (617) 661-1580
M-Sat. 9-9. Sun. 12-8

Same as Cambridge Bread & Circus, but after you cross Mass. Ave., turn right on Bishop Allen Drive to park.

EDGARTOWN (on Martha's Vineyard)
HEALTHY GOURMET NATURAL FOODS
Post Office Triangle, 02539 • (508) 627-7171
Store is easy to find and has everything the Vineyard Haven store has.
M-Sat. 10-5:30 (Summer: 10-6)

Massachusetts

FALMOUTH
AMBER WAVES
310 Dillingham Ave., 02540 • (508) 540-3538
M-Sat. 9-7, Sun. 11-4

From Rte. 28, head west/north on Dillingham and turn right on Rose Morin. First building on left in Dillingham Square.

GARDNER
HAPPY TRAILS
24 Main Street, 01440 • (508) 632-4076
M-W 9-6, Th 9-8, F 9-9, Sat. 9-5, Sun. 12-4

From Rte. 2, take Rte. 68 exit north. Rte. 68 becomes Main St. Store's on right.

GLOUCESTER
CAPE ANNE FOOD CO-OP
26 Emerson Ave., 01930 • (508) 281-0592
M-Sat. 9-7:30, Sun. 12-5

Heading north on Rte. 128, take the first Washington St. exit off the rotary, turn right on Centennial Ave. and right on Emerson Ave. Store is one block down on left.

GREAT BARRINGTON
BERKSHIRE CO-OP MARKET
37 Rossiter Street, 01230 • (413) 528-9697
M-Sat. 9-6 (Th 'til 7:30), Sun. 12-5

From Rte. 7, go west on Rossiter. Store's on left, right in heart of Great Barrington.

GREENFIELD
GREEN FIELDS MARKET (CO-OP)
144 Main Street, 01301 • (413) 773-9567
M-F 8-8, Sat. 9-6, Sun. 10-5

From I-91, take the southern Greenfield exit (of 2) and head into town on Main. Store's on left, west of Rte. 5 and 10 with large green awning.

HADLEY
Bread & Circus
Rte. 9 (Russell St.), 01035 • (413) 586-9932
Sun.- Sun. 9-9

From I-91, take Exit #18 (Northampton) and head north on Rte. 5. Turn right onto Rte. 9 and go about 4 miles. Store is past Rte. 47 on right.

LEVERETT
Village Co-op
180 Rattlesnake Gutter Rd., 01054. • (413) 367-9794
Dar's local co-op. Pizza night on Friday, and a nice staff!
M & Tu. 7-7, W & Th. 7-8, F 7-9, Sat. 9-7, Sun. 9-6

From I-91, take Deerfield exit onto Rte. 116 south about a mile. Turn left on Rte. 47 (watch out for sharp right turn!). Rte. 47 becomes N. Leverett Rd. after you cross Rte. 63. Store's on right. Go down Rattlesnake to park. Store's about 11 miles from I-91.

NEWTON
Bread & Circus
916 Walnut St., 02161 • (617) 769-1141
Sun.-Sun. 9-9

From I-90, take I-95/128 south. Head east on Rte. 9 and just past Dunkin Donuts, take Center Street exit. Bear right at bottom of exit. Turn left on Walnut. Store's on right.

NORTHAMPTON
Cornucopia
150 Main St., 01060 • (413) 586-3800
M-Sat. 9:30-7 (Th & F 'til 9), Sun. 12-5

From I-91, take Exit #18 (Northampton) and head north on Rte. 5. Turn left on Main St. (Rte. 9). Store's on left in the basement of Thornes Market (green awning).

Massachusetts ———————————

ORLEANS
ORLEANS WHOLE FOOD STORE
46 Main St., 02653 • (508) 255-6540
M-Sat. 8:30-6 (F 'til 8), Sun. 10-6

Rte. 6, from east: Take Rte. 6A exit at rotary and turn left on Main St.
Store's on left. From west: Take Rte. 6A exit, turn right on 6A and
right on Main St. Store's on left.

SEEKONK
THE GOOD SEED
138 Central Ave., 02771 • (508) 399-7333
M-Sat. 10-6 (W & Th 'til 8), Sun. 12-5

From I-195, take Newport Ave./Rte. 1A exit towards Pawtucket. Turn
left on Benefit St. Benefit becomes Central. Store's on left on corner of
Central and Rte. 152.

SHREWSBURY
BACK TO BASICS
558 Main St., 01549 • (508) 845-2087
Small on-premises restaurant.
M-Th 9:30-6, F 9:30-7, Sat. 9-5

From south: from I-290, take Exit #22 on to Main St. Store's on right.
From north: take Rte.140 South exit for 1.5 miles. Turn right on Main St.
at first light. Store's on left.

VINEYARD HAVEN (on Martha's Vineyard)
HEALTHY GOURMET NATURAL FOODS
125 State Rd., 02568 • (508) 693-4818
M-Sat. 10-6

From Martha's Vineyard ferry, turn right on State Rd. Store's on right
one mile up.

WELLESLEY
BREAD & CIRCUS
278 Washington St., 02181 • (617) 235-7262
Sun.-Sun. 9-9

From I-95/128 take Rte. 16 West exit. Store's on left, just past intersection of Rte. 16 and Washington.

WILLIAMSTOWN
WILD OATS CO-OP
Colonial Shopping Center, 01267 • (413) 458-8060
Sun.-Sun. 9-6 (Th. 'til 8)

Store's in shopping center on the eastern outskirts of town, on the north side.

WORCESTER
LIVING EARTH
232 Chandler St., 01609 • (508) 753-1896
M-F 9-9, Sat. 9-6, Sun. 11-5

Store's on Rte. 122 (Chandler St.), just south of Rte. 9, on the west side.

Chris, at **Green Fields Market,** Greenfield, Mass.

Photo by: Sarah Davis

MICHIGAN

1. HANCOCK
2. MARQUETTE
3. PETOSKEY
4. TRAVERSE CITY
5. BIG RAPIDS
6. MT. PLEASANT
7. SAGINAW
8. GRAND RAPIDS
9. LANSING AREA
10. WOODLAND
11. KALAMAZOO
12. HILLSDALE
13. ANN ARBOR
14. CANTON
15. DETROIT
16. TROY
17. RICHMOND

ANN ARBOR

PEOPLE'S FOOD CO-OP
212 North 4th Ave., 48104 • (313) 994-9174
M-F 9-9, Sat. 8-7, Sun. 10-8

From I-94, take Ann Arbor/Saline Rd. exit north. Road becomes Main. Turn right on Ann St. and left on 4th. Store's on right.

PEOPLE'S FOOD CO-OP:
740 Packard Rd., 48104 • (313) 761-8173
M-Sat. 9:30-9, Sun. 10-9

From I-94, take State St. exit north for about 2 miles. Turn right on Packard. Store's on right.

WHOLE FOODS
2398 East Stadium Blvd., 48104 • (313) 971-3366
Sun.- Sun. 9-10

From I-94, take US 23 north to Washtenaw/Ann Arbor exit (#37B). Head west on Washtenaw about 2 miles. When, road splits to right, bear left on Stadium. Store's on left in Lamp Post Plaza.

BIG RAPIDS
BIG RAPIDS FOOD CO-OP
220 S. Stewart Street, 49307 • (616) 796-5332
M-F 11:30-6:30, Sat. 10-3

 From Hwy 131, take Rte. 20 and turn right on Maple St.
Turn right on Stewart. Store's on right in the Old Jail.

CANTON
GOOD FOOD CO. WEST
42615 Ford Rd., 48187 • (313) 981-8100
M-Sat. 9-9, Sun. 10-6

From I-275, take Ford Rd. exit west one mile. Store's in Canton
Corners Shopping Ctr. on left.

DETROIT
CASS CORRIDOR CO-OP
4201 Cass, 48201 • (313) 831-7452
M-Th 10-6, F 10-7, Sun. 12-5

 From I-10, take Warren St. exit east.
Turn right on Cass. Store's on right.

EAST LANSING
EAST LANSING FOOD CO-OP
4960 Northwind Dr., 48823 • (517) 337-1266
M-F 10-8, Sat. 9-8, Sun. 12-7

From Hwy 127 take Michigan/Kalamazoo exit. Go east on Michigan Ave.
(becomes Grand River) and turn right on Northwind Dr. Store's on right.

GRAND RAPIDS
EAST TOWN CO-OP
1450 Wealthy St., 49506 • (616) 454-8822
M-F 8-8, Sat. 10-6, Sun. 10-5

From I-96, take Hwy 131 south. Take Wealthy exit off 131 and head
towards town. Store's on right, east of Big Rapids proper, in East Town.

HANCOCK
KEWEENAW CO-OP
1035 Ethel Ave., 49930 • (906) 482-2030
Sun.-Sun. 9-9

Going north on US 41,
turn left on Ethel. Store's 2
blocks down on the right.

HILLSDALE
HILLSDALE FAMILY CO-OP
31 North Broad, 49242 • (517) 439-1397
M-Sat. 9-6 ('til 5:30 in winter). F 'til 7

Rte. 34/99 is Broad St. Store's on east side.

KALAMAZOO
KALAMAZOO PEOPLE'S FOOD CO-OP
436 Burdick, 49007 • (616) 342-5686
M-Sat. 9-7, Sun. 12-5

From I-94, take Westnedge exit north and turn right
on Cedar. Store's on left, corner of Cedar & Burdick.

LANSING
WOLFMOON (CO-OP)
2011 E. Michigan Ave., 48912 • (517) 482-0038
M-F 10-8, Sat. 9-7, Sun. 12-6

From I-96, take I-496 exit (Kalamazoo/Michigan) Get on Rte. 127 north
and take Michigan exit (1st exit). Turn left on Michigan. Store's on right.

MARQUETTE
MARQUETTE ORGANIC FOOD CO-OP
325 West Washington St., 49855 • (906) 225-0671
M-F 10-6, Sat. 10-5

Rte. 41, from either direction, turn/bear left on Washington.

MT. PLEASANT
GREEN TREE GROCERY (CO-OP)
214 North Franklin, 48858 • (517) 772-3221
M-Sat. 9-7

From Hwy 27, take Mt. Pleasant Business 27 exit. Head west on
Broadway, and turn right on North Franklin. Store's on right.

PETOSKEY
GRAIN TRAIN (CO-OP)
421 Howard, 49770 • (616) 347-2381
M, Tu, Th 9-6, W 9-7, F 9-8, Sat. 9-5

From Rte. 131,
131 becomes 31N,
31N becomes Mitchell.
Bear right on Mitchell and turn right on Howard. Store's on the left.

RICHMOND
RAINBOW WAY (CO-OP)
68228 Grand Trunk, 48062 • (313) 727-5475
M-Th 10-6, F 10-8, Sat. 9-5

From I-94, take 26 Mile exit west. Take Gratiot north. Take M 19 north. Turn right on Grand Trunk. Store's on right.

SAGINAW
HERITAGE NATURAL FOODS
717 Gratiot, 48602 • (517) 793-5805
Organic produce in summer only.
M-Sat. 9:30-5:30

From I-75, take Holland Ave. exit (Rte. 46) west. Rte. 46 becomes Gratiot. Store's on left, two blocks past Michigan.

TRAVERSE CITY
ORYANA FOOD CO-OP
601 Randolph St., 49684 • (616) 947-0191
M-Sat. 8-8 (Winter hrs. 9-8), Sun. 12-5

From Rte. 31/37, go east one block on Randolph. Store's on right.

TROY
GOOD FOOD CO. EAST
74 West Maple Rd., 48084 • (313) 362-0886
M-Sat. 9-9, Sun. 10-6

From I-75, take 14 Mile exit west and turn right on Main St. (becomes Livernois). Store's on left, corner of Livernois and 15 Mile (Maple Rd.).

WOODLAND
WOODLAND CO-OP
116 Main, 48897 • (616) 367-4188
M-W 12-5, Sat. 9-12

Store's a half block north of Rte. 43 on Main St.

MINNESOTA

1. BEMIDJI
2. HACKENSACK
3. GRAND RAPIDS
4. VIRGINIA
5. DULUTH
6. BRAINERD

7. BAXTER
8. LONG PRAIRIE
9. ALEXANDRIA
10. MORRIS
11. WILLMAR
12. ST. CLOUD
13. CAMBRIDGE
14. MINNEAPOLIS
15. ST. PAUL
16. BURNSVILLE
17. HASTINGS
18. WINONA
19. ROCHESTER
20. ST. PETER
21. BLUE EARTH

ALEXANDRIA

Village Pantry Food Co-op
2020 Fillmore St., 56308 • (612) 763-4240
M & Sat. 9-6, Tu-F 10-6

From I-94, go north on Rte. 29 towards Alexandria. Turn left at traffic light on 22nd Ave., then make immediate right. Store's on left.

BAXTER

Life Preserver
875 Edgewood Dr., 56401 • (218) 829-7925
Dandelion root tea on tap. "Tastes like coffee!"
M-Sat. 9:30-varies, between 6:30 & 8pm

Store's on Hwy 371, parallel to 371N, on the west side, 1 mile north of The Paul Bunyan Amusement Ctr.

BEMIDJI
Harmony Food Co-op
117 3rd. St. NW, 56601 • (218) 751-2009
M-Sat. 9-7, Sun. 12-5

Co-op worker Greg insists that you'll find it if you go "half a block west of Paul and Babe." Paul and Babe are on Hwy. 197, on the Bemidji waterfront.

BLUE EARTH
Rainbow Food Co-op
103 S. Main St., 56013 • (507) 526-3603
M-F 10-5:30, Sat. 10-5

    From I-90, take Rte. 169 exit south, turn right on 7th and right on Main St. Store's on right.

BRAINERD
Crow Wing Food Co-op
823 Washington St., 56401 • (218) 828-4600
M-F 10-5:30, Sat. 10-4

   Store's 3 blocks east of "the water tower," (intersection of 371 & 210) on 210 (Washington) on left.

BURNSVILLE
Valley Natural Foods Co-op
14015 Grand Ave. South, 55337 • (612) 892-6661
M-Sat. 9-9

From north: off I-35W, take county road 42/ Burnsville Ctr. exit east. Turn left on Nicollet Ave. Turn left on Grand. Store's on right in McAndrew's Center. From south: off I-35, split on to I-35E. Take county road 42 exit and turn left. Turn right on Nicollet. Same as above.

CAMBRIDGE
Mom's Food Co-op
130 2nd Ave. SE, 55008 • (612) 689-4640
M-F 9-5, Sat. 9:30-1:30

    Store's a half block east of Hwy 65 on 2nd Ave. on left.

Minnesota

DULUTH
WHOLE FOODS CO-OP
1332 East 4th St., 55805 • (218) 728-0884
Sun.-Sun. 8-8

From I-35, take Mesaba Ave. exit to 2nd St. Go right on 2nd St. and turn left on 14th Ave. Store's on left, corner of 4th St. and 14th Ave.

GRAND RAPIDS
COVE WHOLE FOODS CO-OP
204 1st Ave. NW, 55744 • (218) 326-1164
M-F 9:30-5:30, Sat. 9:30-3

From Hwy 2, turn south onto NW 1st Ave. Store's on left in Old Mill Place.

HASTINGS
SPIRAL FOOD CO-OP
307 East 2nd St., 55033 • (612) 437-2667
M-Th 9-8, F 9-6, Sat. 9-5, Sun. 11-5

Rte. 61, from north, take first right after bridge, on 3rd. St. Take two quick rights. You'll end on 2nd St. Store's on left. From south, turn right on 3rd before bridge, turn left on Ramsey and right on 2nd. Store's on left.

LONG PRAIRIE
EVERYBODY'S MARKET FOOD CO-OP
11 1st St. N., 56347 • (612) 732-3900
M-F 9-5:30, Sat. 9-5

From Rte. 71, go east on Central about one block. Store's on left, corner of Central and 1st.

MINNEAPOLIS
CAYOL'S NATURAL FOODS
811 La Salle Ave., 55402 • (612) 339-2828
M-F 8:30-6:30, Sat. 8:30-5, Sun. 12-5

Heading downtown, Hwy 55 becomes 8th Street.
Turn south on La Salle. Store's on left, across from Dayton's.

76

MINNEAPOLIS (cont.)
EAST CALHOUN FOOD CO-OP
3255 Bryant Avenue South, 55408 • (612) 827-4145
Sun.-Sun.: 9-9 (Winter 'til 8)

From I-35W, take 35th-36th St. exit. Go west on
36th and turn right on Bryant. Store's on right.

NORTH COUNTRY FOOD CO-OP
2129 Riverside Avenue South, 55454 • (612) 338-3110
M-F 9-9, Sat. 9-8, Sun. 10-8

I-94, from west: take 25th St. exit and turn west on Riverside.
From east: take Riverside exit. Same as above. Store's on left.

SEWARD CO-OP GROCERY
2201 East Franklin Avenue, 55404 • (612) 338-2465
Sun.-Sun. 9-9

From I-94, take Riverside exit south and
turn right on Franklin. Store's on left.

THE WEDGE
2105 Lyndale Avenue South, 55405 • (612) 871-3993
Award-winning, big, famous co-op (but they're all great in Minneapolis)!!
M-F 9am-10pm, Sat. & Sun. 9-9

From I-94, take Lyndale
exit south. Store's on left.

MORRIS
POMME DE TERRE FOOD CO-OP
25 East 7th St., 56267 • (612) 589-4332
Produce by special order only.
M-Sat. 10-6 (Th 'til 8)

From Rte. 28, head south into town on Atlantic.
Turn left on 7th. Store's on left, 2 blocks down.

ROCHESTER
ROCHESTER GOOD FOOD CO-OP
1330 7th St. NW, 55901 • (507) 289-9061
M-F 10-8, Sat. 9-6

From Hwy 52, exit at Civic Center Drive. Turn left on 11th Ave.
and left on 7th St. NW. Store's on left in Northgate Shopping Ctr.

ST. CLOUD
GOOD EARTH FOOD CO-OP
420 St. Germain St. E., 56304 • (612) 253-9290
M-F 9:30-6 (Th 'til 8), Sat. 9:30-5:00

 From I-94, take Washington exit (#75) and head east on Division. Cross river, turn left on Wilson Ave. and left on St. Germain. Store's on left.

ST. PAUL
MISSISSIPPI MARKET (CO-OP)
1810 Randolph Ave., 55105 • (612) 690-0507
M-Sat. 8:30am-9pm, Sun. 10-8

 From I-94, take Snelling Ave. exit south and turn right on Randolph. Store's on left.

ST. PETER
SAINT PETER FOOD CO-OP
100 South Front St., 56082 • (507) 931-4880
M-Sat. 9-7 (F 'til 8), Sun. 11-5

 From Hwy 169, go east on Broadway. Store's on right, corner of B'way & Front.

VIRGINIA
NATURAL HARVEST FOOD CO-OP
119 Chesnut Street, 55792 • (218) 741-4663
M-F 9-6 (Th 'til 8), Sat. 9-5

 From Hwy 169, turn north on Hwy 53 to the first light. Turn right. Turn left on Chesnut. Store's on left.

WILLMAR
KANDI CUPBOARD FOOD CO-OP
412 West Litchfield Ave., 56201 • (612) 235-9477
Organic produce in summer only.
M-F 9-5:30 (Th 'til 8), Sat. 9-5

 From Hwy 12, turn south on 3rd. Turn west on Litchfield. Store's on right.

WINONA
BLUFF COUNTRY FOOD CO-OP
114 E 2nd St., 55987 • (507) 452-1815
M-W 9-6, Th & F 9-8, Sat. 9-6

From I-90, take Hwy 43 exit north about 7 miles. Cross Hwy 61. Road becomes Mankato Ave. Stay on Mankato. Turn left on 2nd. Store's on right.

— L I S T I N G S —

HACKENSACK

Countryside Food Co-op
Box. 262/ Hwy 371, 56452 • (612)675-6865
No produce.
Limited hours (W 10-5, F 1-5, Sat. 9-12)

MISSISSIPPI

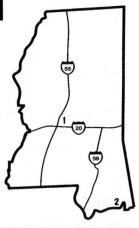

1. JACKSON
2. OCEAN SPRINGS

JACKSON

Rainbow Whole Foods Co-op
4147 Northview Dr., 39206 • (601) 366-1602
M-Sat. 10-6

From I-55, take Meadowbrook Rd. exit west about two miles. Turn right on Northview Dr. Turn left into parking lot of the Dutch Bar. Store is behind that.

OCEAN SPRINGS

Five Seasons Whole Foods Market
601 Washington Ave., 39564 • (601) 875-8882
M-Sat. 9:30-5:30

From I-10, take Exit #50 south on Washington Ave..
Store's on right, past Hwy 90.

MISSOURI

1. KANSAS CITY   3. COLUMBIA
2. INDEPENDENCE   4. ST. LOUIS
                        5. SPRINGFIELD

COLUMBIA
CLOVERS NATURAL FOOD
802 Business Loop 70E, 65201 • (314) 449-1650
Store expanding in 1994.
M-Sat. 9-7, Sun. 12-5

 From I-70, take Rangeline exit south one block and turn right on Business Loop. Store's on left.

KANSAS CITY
WILD OATS
4301 Main Street, 64111 • (816) 931-1873
M-F 8-8, Sat. 8-7, Sun. 10-6

From I-35, take Southwest Trafficway exit south. Turn left on 43rd. Store's on right, corner of 43rd and Main.

INDEPENDENCE
FOOD FAIR CO-OP
16501 East Truman Road, 64050 • (816) 461-8070
M-Sat. 8-8

From I-70 take 291 north to turn right on Truman Rd. Store's on left.

ST. LOUIS
GOLDEN GROCER
335 North Euclid Avenue, 63108 • (314) 367-0405
M-Sat. 10-7, Sun. 12-5

From I-40, take Kings Hwy north. Turn right on Maryland and left on Euclid. Store's on left, set back a bit.

THE NATURAL WAY
8110 Big Bend Blvd., 63119 • (314) 961-3541
M-F 9:30-8, Sat. 9:30-6:30, Sun. 12-5

From I-270, take I-44 exit east. Take Elm exit north one block. Turn right on Big Bend about 5 miles. Store's on right.

THE NATURAL WAY
12345 Olive Blvd., 63141 • (314) 878-3001
M-F 9:30-8, Sat. 9:30-6:30, Sun. 12-5

From I-270, take Olive St. exit. Store is 2 blocks west on right, just north of I-64/40

SPRINGFIELD
EARTHWONDER WHOLEFOODS MARKET
1330 East Battlefield Road, 65804 • (417) 887-5985
Limited organic produce.
M-Sat. 9-7, Sun. 12-5

From I-44, head south on I-65 to Battlefield Rd. Take Battlefield west. Store's on corner of Battlefield and Fremont in Fremont Shopping Ctr.

MONTANA

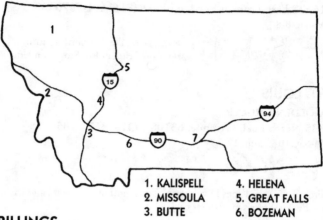

1. KALISPELL
2. MISSOULA
3. BUTTE
4. HELENA
5. GREAT FALLS
6. BOZEMAN
7. BILLINGS

BILLINGS
EVERGREEN HEALTH FOODS
1507 14th St. West, 59102 • (406) 259-4603
M-F 9:30-5:30, Sat. 9:30-5

From I-90, take City Center exit and follow signs to Billings.
Turn right on King Ave, left on 24th St. W., right on Grand Ave.
and left on 14th St. Store's on right in Evergreen Shopping Ctr.

BOZEMAN
COMMUNITY FOOD CO-OP
908 West Main St., 59715 • (406) 587-4039
In the spirit of Bozeman's new glitterati residents, this co-op has an
espresso bar. As for those sub-zero winter temps...
Sun.-Sun. 8am-10pm

From I-90 take Bozeman MSU exit and follow signs to Bozeman. Turn
right onto Main St. Store's on left.

BUTTE
DANCING RAINBOW NATURAL GROCERY
9 South Montana St., 59701 • (406) 723-8811
M-F 10-5:30, Sat. 10-5

From I-90, take Montana exit, head north on Montana
(uphill). Store's on left, next to (natural) Butte Hill Bakery.

GREAT FALLS
2-J's PRODUCE INC.
105 Smelter Ave. NW, 59404 • (406) 761-0134
M-Sat. 9-7

From I-15, take Central Ave exit west about a mile and curve right onto Smelter. Store's on left.

HELENA
REAL FOOD STORE
1090 Helena Ave., 59601 • (406) 443-5150
M-Sat. 9:30-6

 From I-15, take Capital exit and follow signs to Hwy 12 bypass (N. Montana). When bypass becomes Lyndal, take a sharp left on Helena Ave. Store's on right.

KALISPELL
MOUNTAIN VALLEY FOODS
404 1st Ave. East, 59901 • (406) 756-1422
M-Sat. 9-5:30

From Rte. 93, take 4th St. east and turn right on 1st Ave. E. Store's on right.

MISSOULA
GOOD FOOD STORE
920 Kensington Ave., 59801 • (406) 728-5823
M-Sat. 9-8

From I-90, take Orange St. exit south. Orange becomes Stephens. Store's on left, corner of Kensington and Stephens.

FREDDY'S FEED & READ
1221 Helen Ave., 59801 • (406) 549-2127
M-F 7:30am-9pm, Sat. 9-9, Sun. 9-7

From I-90, take Van Buren exit south, turn right on Broadway, left on Madison St., right on University and left on Helen. Store's on right.

NEBRASKA

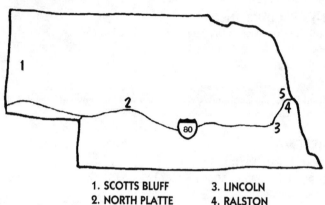

1. SCOTTS BLUFF
2. NORTH PLATTE
3. LINCOLN
4. RALSTON
5. OMAHA

LINCOLN

THE GOLDEN CARROT
6900 O Street, Suite 111, 68510 • (402) 466-5713
M-Sat. 9-9, Sun. 12-5

 Carrot Juice Only

From I-80, take Exit 409 and head west on Cornhusker Hwy. (Hwy 6).
Go south on 84th, then right on O Street. Store's in Meridian Park
Shopping Ctr. on right.

OPEN HARVEST CO-OP
1618 South Street, 68502 • (402) 475-9069
M-Th 9-9, F 9-7, Sat. 9-7, Sun. 11-7

From I-80, take West O Street exit. Take O St. south and turn right on 16th
and go about 20 blocks to South St. Store's on left, corner of 16th and South.

NORTH PLATTE

NATURAL NUTRITION
203 West 6th Street, 69101 • (308) 532-9433
Limited, mostly seasonal organic produce.
M-Sat. 9-5:30

 From I-80, take Rte. 83 exit north and turn left on 5th St. and right
on Vine. Store's on left, corner of Vine and 6th, in a big white house.

OMAHA
COMMUNITY NATURAL FOOD CO-OP
3035 N. 93rd. Street, 68134 • (402) 573-1538
M-Sat. 9:30-6 (Tu 'til 8), Sun. 1-5

From I-80, take I-680 north and head east off Maple St. exit. Turn left
on 93rd. Store's on right.

RALSTON
GRAINERY WHOLE FOODS MARKET & RESTAURANT
7409 Main Street, 68127 • (402) 593-7186
M-F 10-7, Sat. 10-6, Sun. 1-5

From I-80, take 72 St. exit south about 3 miles. Turn right on Main St.
Store's on left.

SCOTTS BLUFF
TAMARAK'S FOODS OF THE EARTH
1613 1st Ave., 69361 • (308) 635-1514
M-Sat 9-5:30 (Th. 'til 7)

From Rte. 26, head west on Overland and right on 1st Ave. Store's on
right in downtown area.

Herb, at **Mt. Hope Natural Foods,** Cottonwood, Arizona – Photo by: Marisa Trubitz

NEVADA

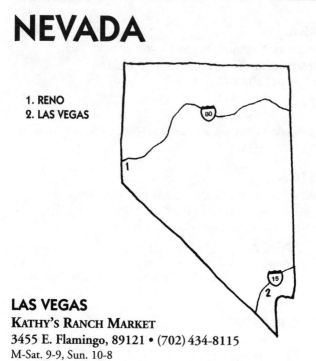

1. RENO
2. LAS VEGAS

LAS VEGAS
KATHY'S RANCH MARKET
3455 E. Flamingo, 89121 • (702) 434-8115
M-Sat. 9-9, Sun. 10-8

From I-15, take E. Flamingo Rd. exit east about 3 miles. Store's on right.

KATHY'S RANCH MARKET
6720 West Sahara, 89102 • (702) 253-7050
M-Sat. 9-9, Sun. 10-8

From I-15, take West Sahara exit about 3.5 miles. Store's on right.

RENO
WASHOE-ZEPHYR FOOD CO-OP
314 Broadway Blvd., 89502 • (702) 323-0391
M-Sat. 9-7, Sun. 11-5

 From I-80, take Wells Ave. south about 2 miles and turn left on Broadway. Store's a half block down.

NEW HAMPSHIRE

1. LITTLETON
2. PLYMOUTH
3. HANOVER
4. KEENE
5. PETERBOROUGH
6. CONCORD
7. MANCHESTER
8. PORTSMOUTH
9. HAMPTON

CONCORD

CONCORD CO-OPERATIVE MARKET

24.5 South Main St., 03301 • (603) 225-6840

M-Th 9-7, Fr 9-8, Sat. 9-6, Sun. 11-5

From I-93, take any Main St. exit. Store's easy to find, in back of a
Mailboxes Etc. store, close to Pleasant St.

GRANITE STATE NATURAL FOODS

164 N. State St., 03301 • (603) 224-9341

M-W 9-7, Th & F 9-8, Sat. 9-6, Sun. 10-5

From I-93, get onto I-393. Turn
right on State St. Store's on right,
with big flora & fauna mural!

HAMPTON

HAMPTON NATURAL FOODS

321 Lafayette Rd., 03842 •(603) 926-5950

Expanding.

M-Sat. 9:30-7, Sun. 12-4

Lafayette is Rte. 1. Store's on east side, just
east of I-95.

New Hampshire

HANOVER
HANOVER CONSUMER CO-OP
45 South Park Street, 03755 • (603) 643-2667
Free coffee samples!
M-F 8-8, Sat. 8-6, Sun. 10-6

 From I-91, take Hanover/Norwich exit
and follow signs to Hanover. Turn right
on Park St. Store's on left.

MANCHESTER
A MARKET
125 Loring Street, 03103 • (603) 668-2650
M-Sat. 9:30-6 (Th & F 'til 9)

From I-293, take S. Willow St. exit (#1) north
about a mile. Turn left on Loring. Store's on left.

PETERBOROUGH
MAGGIE'S MARKETPLACE
14 Main Street, 03458 • (603) 924-7671
M-F 9-6 (Th 'til 7), Sat. 9-5

 From Rte. 101, head north on Grove and
turn right on Main St. Store's on right.

PORTSMOUTH
RISING TIDE
67 Bow Street, 03801 • (603) 431-6833
M-F 9:30-6, Sat. 9:30-5:30, Sun. 11-4

From I-95, take Market St. exit (#7). Follow Market
downtown. Turn left on Bow. Store's on left.

— LISTINGS —

KEENE
THE VITALITY SHOP
116 Main Street, 03431 • (603) 357-3639
No organic produce.

PLYMOUTH
PEPPERCORN NATURAL FOODS
43 Main Street, 03264 • (603) 536-3395
Seasonal produce only.

LITTLETON
MAGOON'S
128 Main Street, 03561 • (603)444-6634
Only organic carrots.

NEW JERSEY

1 CHESTER
2 ROCKAWAY
3 PARSIPPANY
4 MORRISTOWN
5 MONTCLAIR
6 EAST RUTHERFORD
7 EMERSON / RIDGEWOOD
8 NORTH ARLINGTON
9 BAYONNE
10 SCOTCH PLAINS
11 PRINCETON
12 NEW BRUNSWICK
13 LITTLE SILVER
14 POINT PLEASANT BEACH
15 MANAHAWKIN
16 LINDENWOLD / VOORHEES
17 MT. LAUREL

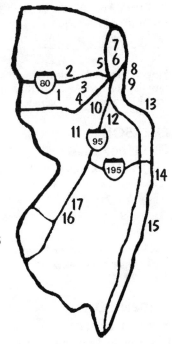

BAYONNE
JOHN'S NATURAL FOODS
486 Broadway, 07002 • (201) 858-0088
M-Sat 9:30-6 (M, Th & F 'til 9)

From NJ Tpk, take Exit 14A and head south on Ave. E. Turn right on 22nd and right on Broadway. Store's on right, about one mile from turnpike.

CHESTER
THE HEALTH SHOPPE
Rte. 206, 07930 • (908) 879-7555
M-F 9-9, Sat. 9-6, Sun. 12-5

Store's on west side of Rte. 206, in Chester Springs Shopping Ctr.

EAST RUTHERFORD
THE THIRD DAY
220 Park Ave., 07073 • (201) 935-4045
M-Tu. 10-6,W-F 10-8, Sat. 10-6

From NJ Tpk, take Exit 16W west on Rte. 3. Take Park Ave. exit and turn right on Park Ave., thru Rutherford. Go around traffic circle and cross RR tracks. Store's on right.

EMERSON
OLD HOOK FARM
650 Old Hook Rd., 07630 • (201) 265-4835
A grocery and a farm!
Tu-Sat. 9-6, Sun. 9-4

Exit 165 off Garden State Pkwy. Head towards Oradell. Turn left on Kinderkamack Rd. and go about 5 miles. Turn right on Old Hook Rd. Store's on left.

LINDENWOLD
NATURAL HEALTH
Blackwood-Clemington & Laurel Rds, 08021 • (609) 784-1021
M-F 9-8, Sat. 10-5, Sun. 12-5

From NJ Turnpike, take Exit 3 (Rte. 168/ Black Horse Pike) south. Turn right on Rte. 42 toward Atlantic City. Take Clemington exit and turn right on Clemington. Store's on left, three miles down.

LITTLE SILVER
HEALTHFAIR
625 Branch Ave., 07739 • (908) 747-3140
M-W 9-6 Th & F 9-7, Sat. 9-6, Sun. 12-5

From Garden State Pkwy, take Redbank/Newman Springs Rd. exit (#109). Take Rte. 520 east. Turn right on Rte. 35, left on White Rd. and right on Branch. Store's 2 miles down on right.

MANAHAWKIN
EARTH GOODS HEALTH FOODS
777 E. Bay Ave., 08050 • (609) 597-7744
M-F 10-7, Sat. 10-6, Sun. 12-5

 From Garden State Pkwy, take Manahawkin exit (#63). Go on Rte. 72 E and north on Rte. 9. Off Rte. 9, turn right on Bay Ave. Soon after, store's on right.

MONTCLAIR
CLAIRMONT HEALTH FOOD CENTER
515 Bloomfield Ave., 07042 • (201) 744-7122
M-Th 9-8, F-Sat 9-7, Sun 12-6

From Garden State Pkway, take Bloomfield exit (#148). Go west on Bloomfield Ave. for about 2 miles. Store's on right.

THE HEALTH SHOPPE
539 Bloomfield Ave., 07042 • (201) 746-3555
M-Th 9-8, F 9-7, Sat. 9-6, Sun. 12-5

From NJ Tpk, take Exit # 15W (I-280 W) and from there, take Mt. Prospect Ave/Verona exit straight 3-4 miles. Bear right on Bloomfield. Store's on left in Louis Harris Building.

MORRISTOWN
THE HEALTH SHOPPE
66 Morris St., 07960 • (201) 538-9131
M-F 9-9, Sat. 9-7, Sun. 9-6

From I-287, take Lafayette exit and follow service road. Turn right on Morris St. at 2nd traffic light (just after Giant Bag & Shop). Store's on right in Midtown Shopping Ctr.

MOUNT LAUREL
GARDEN OF EDEN NATURAL FOODS & COUNTRY KITCHEN INC.
State Hwy. 73 & Ramblewood Pkway., 08054 • (609) 778-1971
M-F 10-9, Sat. 10-6, Sun. 10-3

Take Exit 4 off NJ Tpk. Head south on Rte 73. Store's 1 mile down on left in Ramblewood Center.

New Jersey

NEW BRUNSWICK
GEORGE STREET CO-OP
89 Morris St., 08901 • (908) 247-8280
M-F 10-8, Sat. 10-6, Sun 10-4

 Take Exit 9 off NJ Tpk. Take Rte. 18 north thru 2 lights, and exit right on New Street. At third light, go left on Livingston, then a quick left on to Morris. Store's on left.

NORTH ARLINGTON
SURREY INTERNATIONAL NATURAL FOODS
33 Ridge Rd., 07031 • (201) 991-1905
M-Sat. 10-7:30, Sun. 9-2

From NJ Tpk, take Exit 15W and stay on right. Take Kearny exit straight. Turn right on Schuyler Ave. (first light). Turn left on Belleville Tpk and right on Ridge Rd. Store's on left with a green awning.

PARSIPPANY
THE HEALTH SHOPPE
1123 Rte. 46 East, 07054 • (201) 263-8348
M-F 9-9, Sat. 9-6, Sun. 12-5

From I-80, take Rte. 46/Lake Hiawatha exit west. Store's on left.

POINT PLEASANT BEACH
WILD OATS NATURAL FOODS
1300 Richmond Ave., 08742 • (908) 899-2272
M-Sat. 9:30-6 (F 'til 7), Sun. 12-5

Richmond Ave. is Rte. 35S, and it only goes south. Store's on left.

PRINCETON
WHOLE EARTH CENTER
360 Nassau St., 08540 • (609) 924-7429
M-F 10-7, Sat 10-6

From Rte. 1, head west on Harrison. Make a right at Nassau St. (Rte 27). Store's first driveway on the left.

RIDGEWOOD
Nature's Market Place
1 West Ridgewood Ave., 07450 •(201) 445-9210
M-Sat. 9:30-6 (Th 'til 8)

From Hwy 17, take Ridgewood/Oradell exit and follow signs to
Ridgewood. Pass under train station (becomes W. Ridgewood).
Store's on right.

ROCKAWAY
The Good Food Market & Deli
106 Rte. 46, 07866 • (201) 627-4610
M ,Tu & Th 10-7, W & F 10-7:30, Sat. 10-6, Sun. 11-4

I-80, from east: take Parsippany/Morris Plains/ Rte. 46 exit (#42).
Veer off to right on Cherry Hill Rd. (road ends). Turn left on Rte. 46.
Store's 4 miles down on right.

SCOTCH PLAINS
Autumn Harvest Health Foods
1759 East 2nd St. 07076 • (908) 322-2130
M-F 9:30-6, Thurs. 'til 7:30, Sat. 9:30-5

From Hwy. 22, go south on Park Ave., then turn left on 2nd St. Store's
on the right.

VOORHEES
Richard's Natural Foods
10 White Horse Road • (609) 627-5057
The store's attached to a macrobiotic restaurant.
Sun.-Sun. 11:30-2:30, M-Sat. +5-9, Sun. +4-8

From NJ Tpk take Exit #4 and head north on Rte. 73. Take Hwy 295
south and take Vorhees/Haddonfield / Rte. 561 exit (same exit if heading north on Hwy 295). Turn left at top of ramp and right on Burnt
Mill Rd. Store's on left.

NEW MEXICO

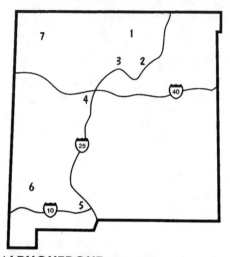

1 TAOS
2 LAS VEGAS
3 SANTA FE
4 ALBUQUERQUE
5 LAS CRUCES
6 SILVER CITY
7 FARMINGTON

ALBUQUERQUE
LA MONTANITA FOOD CO-OP
3500 Central SE, 87106 • (505) 265-4631
M-Sat. 8:30am-9pm, Sun. 8:30-8

From I-40, take Carlisle exit south about 2 miles. Store's on right, corner
of Central and Carlisle in the Nob Hill Shopping Center.

WILD OATS
6300-A San Mateo NE, 87109 • (505) 823-1933
Sun.-Sun. 8 am-11pm

From I-25, take San Mateo exit. Head south on San Mateo. Store's
about 100 yards down in Far North Shopping Center.

FARMINGTON
WILDLY NATURAL FOODS
3030 E. Main St., Suite M, 87401 • (505) 326-6243
M-Sat. 9-6

   Rte. 64 becomes Main St. in Farmington.
Store's on north side.

LAS CRUCES

ORGAN MOUNTAIN FOOD CO-OP
1300 El Paseo St., Suite M, 88001 • (505) 523-0436
M-Sat. 8-8, Sun. 9-6

From I-25, take Hwy 70 exit west towards Las Cruces (becomes Main).
Turn left on El Paseo. Store's on right at light in Idaho Crossings
Shopping Center.

LAS VEGAS

SEMILLA NATURAL FOODS
510 University Ave., 87701 • (505) 425-8139
M-F 10-6, Sat. 10-4

 From I-25, take University exit (2nd Las Vegas
exit) west. Store's on right.

SANTA FE

THE MARKETPLACE
627 West Alameda, 87501 • (505) 984-2852
M-Sat. 7:30am-9pm, Sun. 9-8

From I-25, take St. Francis exit north about 3 miles and turn right on
Alameda. Store's on left.

WILD OATS
1090 St. Francis Dr., 87501 • (505) 983-5333
Sun.-Sun. 8am-11pm

From I-25, take St. Francis Drive exit. Store's about 3 miles up on left.

WILD OATS
1708 Llano St. "B," 87501 • (505) 473-4943
Sun.-Sun. 8am-10pm

From I-25, take Cerrillos Rd. exit (one direction). Turn right on St.
Michael's. Store's on right, corner of St. Michael's and Llano.

New Mexico ────────────────────

SILVER CITY
Silver City Food Co-op
520 North Bullard Street, 88061 • (505) 388-2343
Store's in an area with museums, coffee shops, etc.
M-F 9-6, Sat. 9-5

From Rte. 180, head south on Hudson, turn right on College and left
on Bullard St. Store's on left.

TAOS
Amigo's Natural Grocery
326 South Santa Fe, 87571 • (505) 758-8493
M-Sat. 9-7, Sun. 11-5

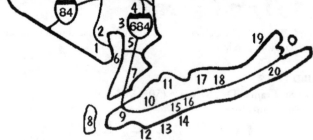

Store's on Hwy 64 (Santa Fe), three lights south of Taos Plaza, on the west side.

NEW YORK METRO

1. CHESTNUT RIDGE
2. NEW CITY
3. PEEKSKILL
4. MAHOPAC
5. NORTHERN
   WESTCHESTER
   A. KATONAH
   B. MT. KISCO
   C. PLEASANTVILLE

6. SOUTHERN
   WESTCHESTER
   A. WHITE PLAINS
   B. SCARSDALE
7. MANHATTAN
8. STATEN ISLAND
9. BROOKLYN
10. QUEENS
11. GLEN COVE
12. OCEANSIDE

13. BALDWIN
14. SEAFORD/
    MASSAPEQUA
15. HICKSVILLE
16. PLAINVIEW
17. HUNTINGTON
18. COMMACK
19. PORT JEFFERSON
20. RIVERHEAD

NEW YORK

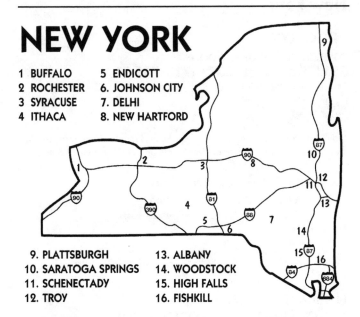

1 BUFFALO
2 ROCHESTER
3 SYRACUSE
4 ITHACA

5 ENDICOTT
6. JOHNSON CITY
7. DELHI
8. NEW HARTFORD

9. PLATTSBURGH
10. SARATOGA SPRINGS
11. SCHENECTADY
12. TROY

13. ALBANY
14. WOODSTOCK
15. HIGH FALLS
16. FISHKILL

ALBANY
HONEST WEIGHT FOOD CO-OP
112 Quail Street, 12206 • (518) 465-0383
M & Tu 10-6:30, W-F 10-8, Sat. 10-6, Sun. 12-5

I-90, from west: take Everett Road exit south into city, turn left on Central Ave. and left on Quail. Store's on right.
From east: take Rte. 9 South exit, turn right on Central and right on Quail. Store's on right.

MILES NATURAL FOODS
28 Central Ave., 12206 • (518) 462-1020
Certified herbalist on staff; ask for Susan if you need an appointment!
M-F 10-6:30 (Th 'til 8), Sat. 10-6, Sun 12-5

From I-90, take Arborhill exit and go five lights south on Henry Johnson/Northern Blvd. Turn left on Central "and park."

BALDWIN
THE HUMAN BEAN (CO-OP)
995 Church Street, 11510 • (516) 379-0183
M-Sat. 10-4:45 (Tu & Th 'til 7:30). July & Aug., Sat. 10-1

From Southern State Pkwy, take Meadowbrook to M-9W
(Freeport Merrick Rd) and take it. Turn left on Milburn Ave. and right on Church. Store's on right.

New York ────────────

BROOKLYN

APPLETREE NATURAL FOODS
7911 3rd Ave., 11209 • (718) 745-5776
M-F 9:30-6:30 (Th 'til 7:30), Sat. 9:30-6

Store's in Bay Ridge area. From I-278, take Ft. Hamilton exit onto 4th Ave.
Turn left on Shore and right on 3rd. Store's on right, between 79 & 80.

BACK TO THE LAND NATURAL FOODS
142 7th Ave. , 11215 • (718) 768-5654
Store's expanding. It's been around for 24 years!
Sun.-Sun. 9-9

Store's 2 blocks west of Prospect
Park, near Garfield Place.

Flatbush Food Co-op
1318 Cortelyou Rd., 11226 • (718) 284-9717
M-F 9:30-8, Sat. & Sun. 9:30-7

From Ocean Pkwy, head east on Cortelyou.
Store's two blocks from D train Cortelyou stop.

BUFFALO

LEXINGTON REAL FOODS CO-OP
230 Lexington Ave., 14222 • (716) 884-8828
Near Elmwood, "The hip street in Buffalo."
Sun.- Sun. 9-9

From I-90, take Rte. 33 exit west, exit on East Ferry and go west.
Turn left on Elmwood and right on Lexington. Store's on left.

NORTH BUFFALO FOOD CO-OP
3144 Main St., 14214 • (716) 836-8058
M-Sat. 9-9, Sun. 10-6

From I-90, turn north on I-290 and take Main St. exit west about a
mile. Store's on right.

CHESTNUT RIDGE
HUNGRY HOLLOW CO-OP
841 Chestnut Ridge Rd., 10977 • (914) 356-3319

M-Sat. 10-6

From Garden State Pkwy heading north, take last NJ exit (#172). Turn left and then turn right on Chestnut Ridge Rd. Store's on left.

COMMACK
THE MUNG BEAN
6522 Jericho Turnpike, 11725 • (516) 499-2362

M-Th 9-8, F 9-8, Sat. 9-6, Sun. 11-5

From LIE, take Commack Rd. exit (#52) and head north to Jericho Tpk. Store's in Commack Corners Shopping Ctr., corner of Commack Rd. and Jericho Tpk.

DELHI
GOOD CHEAP FOOD (CO-OP)
53 Main St., 13753 • (607) 746-6562

M-Sat. 10-5 (F 'til 6)

Rte 28, from north: Main St. is also Rte. 28 for awhile. STAY on Main St. Store's on left. From south: turn left on Main St. Store's on left.

ENDICOTT
DOWN TO EARTH WHOLE FOODS CO
305 Grant Ave., 13760 • (607) 785-2338

M-F 9-9, Sat. 10-6, Sun. 12-6

From Hwy 17 take Endicott exit and get on Rte. 26 (north). Take ramp onto overpass where sign says Owego. Grant Ave. is the first left. Store's on left.

FISHKILL
JOIE DE VIE HEALTH EMPORIUM
Rte. 9, 12524 • (914) 298-7986

Tu- F 10-6 (Th 'til 7), Sun. 10-6

From I-84, take Rte. 9 Poughkeepsie exit. Store's exactly three miles north on left, in Market Square & Lawrence Farms.

GLEN COVE
RISING TIDE NATURAL MARKET
42 Forest Ave., 11542 • (516) 676-7895
M-Sat. 9-7, Sun. 10-6

From Rte. 25A, take Glen Cove Road north to the end and turn right. Store's five traffic lights down on right.

HICKSVILLE
GOOD LIFE NATURAL FOODS
339 South Broadway, 11801 • (516) 935-5073
The store may be moving in mid-1994. Phone number will stay the same.
M-F 9-7, Sat. 10-5

From LIE, take Exit #41S. Stay on Rte. 107 about 2 miles. Store's on left.

HIGH FALLS
HIGH FALLS FOOD CO-OP
1098 State Road 213, 12440 • (914) 687-7262
M-Sat. 10-7, Sun. 10-6

Store's on corner of Lucas Ave. and Rte. 213.

HUNTINGTON
SWEET POTATOES ORGANIC MARKET & PEOPLE'S CO-OP
35B Gerard St., 11743 • (516) 423-6424
M-W 9:30-7, Th & F 9:30-9, Sat. 9:30-7, Sun. 12-5

Rte. 25A becomes Main St. in Huntington. Turn north on Wall St. and right on Gerard. Store's on left.

ITHACA
GREENSTAR CO-OP
701 West Buffalo St., 14850 • (607) 273-9392
M-F 10-9, Sat. & Sun. 10-7

Store is about 8 blocks from Oasis, half a mile from downtown center.

ITHACA (cont.)
OASIS
215 North Cayuga, DeWitt Mall, 14850 • (607) 273-8213
This store bakes the bread for the Moosewood Restaurant, down the hall!
M-Sat. 9:30-6 (Th & F 'til 7), Sun. 12-5

From Rte. 13 take Buffalo St. east. Mall's on right corner of Buffalo and Cayuga, maroon awning.

JOHNSON CITY
HEALTH BEAT NATURAL FOODS
214 Main St., 13790 • (607) 797-1001
M & Th 9-9, Tu, W & F 9-7, Sat. 10-6, Sun. 12-5

From I-81, take Johnson City exit and head east on Main. Store's on right.

KATONAH
KATONAH NATURAL MARKET
202 Katonah Ave., 10538 • (914) 232-7574
M-Sat. 10-6 (W & Sat. 'til 7), Sun 12-5

Saw Mill Pkwy, take Katonah exit. From south: follow signs to Harris Rd. Turn left on Harris, right on Bedford Rd. (117) and bear right on Katonah Ave. Store's on right. From north: turn right onto Bedford (117). Same as above.

MAHOPAC
THE NATURAL SELECTION LTD.
Lake Plaza Shopping Ctr., 10541 • (914) 628-0533
M-F 10-6 (W & Th 10-8), Sat. 9-6, Sun. 11-5

From I-84, take Exit #19 and turn right off ramp onto Rte. 312 towards Carmel. Turn right at first light. Turn left on Rte. 6. Store's about 5 miles down on left in Lake Plaza Shopping Ctr.

MANHATTAN

*Since NYC is basically a big numbered grid and most people don't drive there, the cross streets are given, but not full directions. By all means, spend a buck or two and get a small map!!

COMMODITIES EAST
165 1st Ave., 10003 • (212) 260-2600
Sun.-Sun. 10-9

Cross street is 10th St.

COMMODITIES NATURAL
117 Hudson, 10013 • (212) 334-8330
Expanding.
Sun.-Sun.10-8

 On Hudson, at Northmore (Franklin stop on the 1 or 9 subway).

DOWN TO EARTH
33 7th Ave., 10011 • (212) 924-2711
M-F 9am-9:30pm, Sat. 10-8:30, Sun. 11:30-8:30

 Store's between 12th and 13th.

GOOD EARTH FOODS
1334 1st Ave., 10021 • (212) 472-9055
M-F 9:30-7:30, Sat. 9:30-6:30, Sun. 12-6

Store's between 71 and 72 St.

GOOD EARTH FOODS
169 Amsterdam Ave., 10023 • (212) 496-1616
All the same as the other store. Store's at 68th St.

THE HEALTH NUTS
1208 2nd Ave., 10021 • (212) 593-0116
M-Sat. 9:30-8:30, Sun. 12-7

Store's between 63 and 64 St.

MANHATTAN (cont.)

THE HEALTH NUTS
2611 Broadway, 10025 • (212) 678-0054
Expanding.
M-Sat. 9-8:45, Sun. 11-7

 Store's between 98 and 99 St.

THE HEALTH NUTS
2141 Broadway, 10023 • (212) 724-1972
M-Sat. 9-8, Sun 11-7

 Store's between 75 and 76 St.

HEALTHY PLEASURES
93 University Place, 10003 • (212) 353-FOOD
M-Th 7am-10pm, F 7am-11pm, Sat. & Sun. 8am-11pm

Store's between 11 and 12 St. This one's new and very clean, as well as on the big side.

INTEGRAL YOGA
229 West 13th St., 10011 • (212) 243-2642
M-F 10-9:30, Sat. 10-8:30, Sun. 12-6:30

Store's between 7th and 8th Ave., near Down to Earth. Both great stores!

NATIVE FARM ORGANICS
332 East 11th St., 10003 • (212) 614-0727
"NYC's only all-organic food store." Nothing but produce at this store.
Sun.-Sun. 10-10

Store's between 1st & 2nd Ave.

PRANA FOODS
125 1st Ave., 10003 • (212) 982-7306
M-Sat. 10-8, Sun. 11-7

 Store's between 7 St. and St. Marks (8th St.).
St. Mark's Place is young, hip and trendy.

MANHATTAN (cont.)

Sunrise Natural Foods
142 West Houston, 10012 • (212) 254-4373
M-Sat. 10-10, Sun. 11-10

 Cross street is MacDougal. In the
heart of Greenwich Village.

Whole Foods Natural Supermarket
117 Prince St. • (212) 982-1000
M-F 8am-10pm, Sat. & Sun. 9am-10pm

Store's between
Greene and Wooster.

MT. KISCO

Good Earth Health Foods
13 Main St., 10549 • (914) 241-3500
M-F 9-6:30, Sat. 9:30-5:30

 From Saw Mill River Pkwy, take
Kisco Ave. exit. Turn left on Kisco
and left on Rte. 133. Store's on left.

NEW CITY

Back to the Earth
306A South Main St., 10956 • (914) 634-3511
M-F 9-7:30, Sat. 9-6, Sun. 11-5

From I-87, take Palisades Pkwy exit north (#13N). From Palisades, take
Exit #10 and turn left off ramp. Turn right on Little Tor Road for about
1.5 miles. Turn right on Collyer and left on Main. Store's on right.

NEW HARTFORD

Peter's Cornucopia
52 Genesee St. • (315) 724-4998
M-F 9:30-8, Sat. 9:30-6, Sun.12-5 (Sun. closed in July & Aug.)

From I-90, take Genessee exit and go on S. Genessee for about three
miles. Store's on right.

OCEANSIDE
JANDI'S NATURE WAY, INC.
24 Atlantic Ave. • (516) 536-5535
M-Sat. 10-6 (F 'til 9), Sun. 12-4

From Rte. 27, go south on Longbeach Rd. Store's in Great Lincoln Shopping Center on right, corner of Atlantic and Longbeach.

PEEKSKILL
ODESSA NUTRITIONAL CENTER
The Beach Shopping Center, 10566 • (914) 737-1422
M-Sat. 9-6 (Th & F 9-7)

From Taconic State Pkwy, take Peekskill exit and head west on Rte. 202 about 4 miles. Store's on right.

PLAINVIEW
DR. B. WELL NATURALLY
8 Washington Avenue, 11803 • (516) 932-9355
M-F 10-8, Sat. 10-7, Sun. 11-7

LIE, from west: take Exit #45 and take Manetto Hill Rd. south. Turn left on Washington. Store's on left. From east: take Exit #48 and turn left on Round Swamp Road. Bear right on Old Country, turn right on Manetto Hill Road and right on Wash. Store's on right.

PLATTSBURGH
NORTH COUNTRY CO-OP
13 City Hall Place, 12901 • (518) 561-5904
M 10-4, Tu-F 10-7, Sat. 10-4

Take Exit 37 (Plattsburgh/Rte. 3) east and follow signs to Rte. 9, Plattsburgh and historic district. Store's right next to City Hall.

PLEASANTVILLE
WAY OF LIFE NATURAL FOODS CO-OP
503A Bedford Rd., 10570 • (914) 769-4332
M-Sat. 10-5 (Tu & Th 'til 8), Sun 1-5

Saw Mill River Pkwy, from south: take Bedford Road exit and turn right. Store's in small shopping center on left. From north: take Manville Rd./Pleasantville exit. Turn right at light and take first right. Store's on right.

PORT JEFFERSON
PROVISIONS
156 East Main St., 11777 • (516) 474-0163
M 9-5, Tu-F 9-7, Sat. 8-6, Sun. 8-5

Main St. is 25A. Store's one block east of Main.
Pt. Jefferson's a stop for Bridgeport Ferry.

QUEENS
QUEENS HEALTH EMPORIUM
159-01 Horace Harding Exp., 11365 • (718) 358-6500
M-Sat. 10-8, Sun. 11-6

LIE: from west, take Exit 24 and head for 164th St. Make a full U-
turn. Store's on corner of 159th and Horace Harding Exp. From east:
take Exit 24, store's right there, on right.

QUANTUM LEAP NATURAL GROCERY
65-60 Fresh Meadow Lane, 11365 • (718) 762-3572
Restaurant attached.
M 10-8, Tu-Sun. 10-10 (F & Sat.'til 11)

From LIE take Exit 25 and go two blocks south. Turn right on
67th Ave. Store's on right, corner of 67th and Fresh Meadow.

RIVERHEAD
THE GREEN EARTH GROCERY
50 East Main St., 11901 • (516)369-2233
M-Th 9-7, F 9-8, Sat. 10-6, Sun. 10-2

Rte. 25 becomes Main St. through Riverhead. Store's on left.

ROCHESTER
GENESEE CO-OP FOODSTORE
713 Monroe Ave., 14607 • (716) 244-3900
M-F 10-7 (Th 'til 8), Sat. 10-6, Sun. 10-4:30

From Rte. 490 take Monroe Ave. exit west two blocks.
Store's on left, one mile east of downtown.

SARATOGA SPRINGS
Saratoga Whole Foods Store & Co-op
51 Ash Street, 12866 • (518) 587-6840
Tu 10-4, W-F 9:30-6, Sat. 10-4, Sun. 1-4

 From I-87, take Exit 13N and come into town on Rte. 9. Turn left on 29 (Washington), and left on Beekman. Store's on left, corner of Beekman and Ash.

Four Seasons Natural Foods Store & Café
33 Phila St., 12866 • (518) 584-4670
Store has a buffet restaurant.
M-Th 10-6:30, F & Sat. 10-8:30, Sun. 9:30-5

From I-87, take Exit 15. Go south on Rte. 9 about 2 miles. Turn left on Phila St. Store's on left.

SCARSDALE
Mrs. Green's Natural Market
365 Central Park Ave., 10583 • (914) 472-9675
M 9-8, Tu-Sat. 9-7, Sun. 11-6

I-287, take Exit 5. From east: and turn left off exit, left on Tarrytown Rd. (Rte. 119) and right on 100S (Central Park Ave.). Store's on right. From west: go right on Rte. 119. Same as above.

SEAFORD/MASSAPEQUA
Earth Harvest
1244 Hicksville Rd. • (516) 797-0700
M-Sat. 9:30-7, Sun. 11-5

From Southern State Pkwy, take Exit 29 (Exit 29S from west) south on Rte. 107. Store's on right in Calvert Shopping Center.

SCHENECTADY
Earthly Delights
162 Jay St. • (518) 372-7580
M-Sat. 9-5:30 (Th 'til 9:30)

From I-90 take Exit 26 and follow signs to Schenectady. Road becomes I-890, which dumps you right on Broadway. Take right on State. There's no driving on Jay St. Street's on left.

STATEN ISLAND
Tastebuds Natural Foods
1807 Hylan Blvd., 10305 • (718) 351-8693
M-Sat. 9:30-8:30, Sun. 12-6:30

I-278, from Brooklyn: take Hylan Blvd. exit and get on Richmond Rd.
Turn left on Buel and right on Hylan. Store's on right. From Jersey: Take
Clove Rd./Richmond Rd. exit and turn right on Richmond. Same as above.

SYRACUSE
Real Food Co-op
618 Kensington Road, 13210 • (315) 472-1385
M-F 11-8, Sat. 8-6 ('til 8 in Winter), Sun. 12-6

 From I-81, take Adams St. exit, and take E. Adams
St. east and turn right on Ostrom Ave. then left on
Euclid. Turn right on Westcott 3 blocks, then left on Kensington Rd. Store's on right.

TROY
Uncle Sam's Good Natural Products
77 4th Street, 12180 • (518) 271-7299
M-F 10-6, Sat. 10-4

From I-87, take Rte. 7 exit east. Take Downtown Troy exit, which will put
you on 6th St. south. Turn right on Congress and right on 4th. Store's on left.

WHITE PLAINS
Manna Foods Inc.
171 Mamaroneck Ave., 10601 • (914) 946-2233
M & F 9-6, Tu -Th 9-7, Sat. 9-5 (Kitchen M-F 11:30-2:30)

From Hutch. River Pkwy: take Exit # 23N. Store's 4-5 miles up on right.

WOODSTOCK
Sunflower Natural Foods
Bradley Meadows Shopping Center, 12498 • (914)
M-Sat. 9-9, Sun. 10-7

I-87, from south: take Rte. 28 exit (#19) west about 5 miles, then turn right on
Rte. 375 (to the end) and left on Rte. 212. Store's on right. From north: take
Saugerties exit (# 20), and take Rte. 212 west about 8 miles. Store's on right.

NORTH CAROLINA

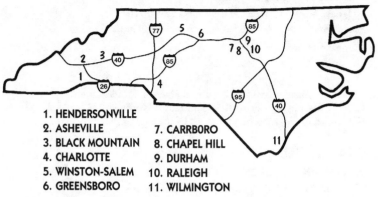

1. HENDERSONVILLE
2. ASHEVILLE
3. BLACK MOUNTAIN
4. CHARLOTTE
5. WINSTON-SALEM
6. GREENSBORO
7. CARRBORO
8. CHAPEL HILL
9. DURHAM
10. RALEIGH
11. WILMINGTON

ASHEVILLE

EARTH FARE
66 Westgate Pkwy, 28806 • (704) 253-7656
M-Sat. 9-9, Sun. 10-7

Store's on west side of I-240 loop (Westgate Pkwy), on north/west side of street.

FRENCH BROAD CO-OP
90 Biltmore Ave., 28801 • (704) 255-7650
M-F 9-8, Sat. 9-7, Sun. 1-6

From anywhere, follow signs to downtown Asheville. Store's 2 blocks south of Vance Monument.

BLACK MOUNTAIN

HEALTHY HARVEST
115 Black Mountain Ave., 28711 • (704) 669-9813
M-Th 9:30-5:30, F & Sat. 10-6

From I-40, take further west of two Black Mountain exits (#64) and go north. Turn left on Vance Ave. Store's on right.

CARRBORO
WEAVER ST. MARKET
101 East Weaver St., 27510 • (919) 929-0010
Renowned cook Rob Nichols works here and bakes bread 6 times a week!
M-F 9-9, Sat. 9-8, Sun. 10-8

From I-40, take Bypass 15-501 south to Hwy 54. Head west on 54.
Take Greensboro St. exit north one mile. Store's on right in Carr Mill
Mall, corner of Greensboro and Weaver, by the huge (organic) pecan trees.

CHAPEL HILL
WELLSPRING GROCERY
81 South Elliott Rd., 27514 • (919) 968-1983
Sun.-Sun. 9-9, Café: 7:30am-8pm, Sun. 7:30-2:30

Rte. 15/501 intersects with Elliott about 2 miles west of Chapel Hill.
Store's on left.

CHARLOTTE
*The people who work in these stores are very supportive of the other
stores. That's a sign of a thriving natural food community!*

BERRYBROOK FARM NATURAL FOOD PANTRY
1257 East Blvd., 28203 • (704) 334-6528
M-Sat. 9:30-6 (Deli open 11-4)

Same street as Talley's (see below), corner of East Blvd. and
Kennilworth.

PEOPLE'S NATURAL FOOD MARKET
617 South Sharon Amity Rd., 28211 • (704) 364-3891
M-Sat. 9:30-6

From I-77, take I-277 exit and take 4th St. exit. Go south on 4th St
(becomes Randolph) and turn right on Sharon Amity Rd. Store's on left.

CHARLOTTE (cont.)
T<small>ALLEY'S</small> G<small>REEN</small> G<small>ROCERY</small>
1408-C East Blvd., 28203 • (704) 334-9200
M-Sat 9-9, Sun. 10-7

From I-277, take Kennilworth exit away from town and to East Blvd.
Turn left on East. Store's on the right in the Dilworth Gardens
Shopping Center, about a block down.

DURHAM
W<small>ELLSPRING</small> M<small>ARKET</small>
737 9th St., 27705 • (919) 286-0371
9th St. is "groovy," says store manager and fellow travelers.
M-Sat. 9-9, Sun. 10-8

From I-85, take Hillsborough exit south. Turn left on Club Blvd and
right on 9th St. Store's on right.

GREENSBORO
D<small>EEP</small> R<small>OOTS</small> C<small>O-OP</small>
3728 Spring Garden, 27407 • (919) 292-9216
M-F 10-7:30, Sat. 9-7, Sun. 12-6

From I-40, take Wendover exit and head north/east off ramp. 500 feet
down, turn left on Spring Garden. Store's on left.

HENDERSONVILLE
L<small>IFE'S</small> B<small>EST</small> M<small>ARKET</small> (C<small>O-OP</small>)
715B Old Spartanburg Hwy, 28792 • (704) 693-0505
M-F 10-6, Sat. 10-5

From Hwy 25, take Barnwell exit east. Turn right on Spartanburg
Hwy. Store's on right.

North Carolina

RALEIGH

NOAH'S CO-OP GROCERY
745 West Johnson St., 27603 • (919) 834-5056
"Largest selection of organic produce in North Carolina!"
M-F 10-8, Sat. 10-6, Sun. 1-6

From north side of I-40 Beltline, take Capitol Blvd. exit toward down-town, turn right on Peace St., take first light left on West St. and turn right on W. Johnson. Store's on left.

WELLSPRING GROCERY
3540 Wade Ave., 27607 • (919) 828-5805
Sun.-Sun. 9-9

Store's one block east of I-40 beltline, on left in the Ridgewood Shopping Center.

WILMINGTON

TIDAL CREEK FOODS, INC. (CO-OP)
4406 Wrightsville Ave., 28403 • (919) 799-2667
M-F 10-6 (Th 'til 8), Sat. 10-5

 I-40 becomes College Road (Hwy 132). Take right on Wrightsville Ave. Store's on left.

DOXIE'S MARKET
1319 Military Cutoff Rd., 28403 • (919) 256-9952
M-Sat. 9-7, Sun. 1-6

Hwy 74/76 becomes Oleander Dr. Stay on Oleander (becomes Military Cutoff) Store's on right in Landfall Ctr.

WINSTON-SALEM

FRIENDS OF THE EARTH
114 Reynolda Village, 27106 • (919) 725-6781
M-F 10-7, Sat. 10-5

From I-40, take Silas Creek Pkwy exit north. Turn right on Reynolda Road. Turn left into the byway of Reynolda Village. Store is in a barn.

NORTH DAKOTA

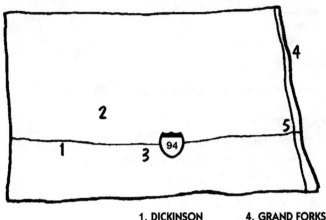

1. DICKINSON   4. GRAND FORKS
2. BEULAH   5. FARGO
3. BISMARCK

BEULAH

Terry's Health Products
218 West Main St., 58523 • (701) 873-2596
M-F 10-5, Sat. 10-3

From Hwy 49, take Main St. three blocks east. Store's on left in Galloway Square.

BISMARCK

Terry's Health Products
717 East Main Ave., 58501 • (701) 223-1026
M-F 9-6, Sat. 10-5

From I-94, take Hwy 83 exit south. Turn left on Main Ave. Store's on right.

Storefront Food Co-op
609 Memorial Hwy, 58504 • (701) 255-7757
M-W 12-6, F 12-6, Sat. 11-3

From I-94, take one of the Bismarck exits south into town. Turn west on Main. Head west toward river. Turn left on Washington and right on Memorial Hwy. Store's on left.

DICKINSON
NATURAL HEALTH
Rte. 22, 58601 • (701) 225-6614
No produce.
M-F 9-6, Sat. 9-5

From I-94 take Rte. 22 exit south. Store's on right.

FARGO
SWANSON HEALTH PRODUCTS
109 North Broadway, 58102 •(701) 293-9842
Seasonal organic produce.
M 9-8, T-F 9-6, Sat. 9-5

From I-94, take University Dr. exit north. Turn east on 2nd Ave. and left on Broadway. Store's on left.

TOCHI PRODUCTS
1111 2nd Ave. North, 58102 • (701) 232-7700
M-Sat. 10-6 (Th 'til 8)

From I-94, take Main Ave. exit to 10 St. (one way north). Turn left on 2nd Ave. Store's on right in old train depot.

GRAND FORKS
GRAND FORKS FOOD CO-OP
1602 9th Ave. North, 58203 • (701) 775-4542
M-Sat. 10-6 (Th 'til 8)

From Hwy 2, turn south on N. Washington and right on 9th Ave. North. Store's on right.

OHIO

1 TOLEDO
2 CLEVELAND/
  MIDDLEBURG HEIGHTS   3 AKRON

4 KENT
5 YOUNGSTOWN
6 WOOSTER
7 COLUMBUS
8 DAYTON
9 CINCINNATI

AKRON
CO-OPERATIVE MARKET
590 West Market St., 44303. • (216) 762-2667
M-Sat. 10-6 (Th & F 'til 8), Sun. 12-5

From I-77, take Rte. 59 & Downtown exit. Turn left on Exchange St. and right on Rhodes. Store's on right, corner of Rhodes and W. Market.

MUSTARD SEED MARKET
3885 West Market St., 44333 • (216) 666-7333
M-Th 9-9, F & Sat. 9am-10pm, Sun. 10-6

From I-77, take Market St. (Rte. 18) east to Fairlawn. Store's on left in West Market Plaza.

CINCINNATI
CLIFTON NATURAL FOODS
207 West McMillan • (513) 651-5288
M-Sat. 10-7, Sun. 11-4

From I-75, take Hopple St. exit and bear left at Dixmith Ave. until it ends. Turn right on Clifton until it ends and turn left on McMillan. Store's on right.

NEW WORLD FOOD SHOP
347 Ludlow Ave., 45220 • (513) 861-1101
Very little organic produce.
M-Sat. 11-8:30, Sun. 11-7

From I-75, take Hopple St. exit and go left on Hopple. Turn left on Central Pkwy and bear to the right. Road becomes Ludlow. Store's on right.

CLEVELAND
FOOD CO-OP
11702 Euclid Ave., 44106 • (216) 791-3890
M-Sat. 9-8, Sun. 10-6

From I-90 take Martin Luther King exit south and turn left on Euclid. Store's in University Circle Area, about a half mile up on right.

NORTHWEST NATURAL AND SPECIALTY FOODS
1636 Northwest Blvd. • (614)488-0607
M-Sat. 9-8, Sun. 11-6

From I-70, take Grandview exit and follow Grandview. Turn right on King. Store's on left.

COLUMBUS
BEXLEY NATURAL FOOD CO-OP
508 North Cassady Ave., 43209 • (614) 252-3951
M-F 9-8, Sat. 9-6, Sun. 12-5

From I-70, take Bexley exit and take Alum Creek Drive (one direction). Turn right on Main and left on Cassady. Store's on right.

116

DAYTON
WORLD OF NATURAL FOODS
2314 Far Hills Ave. • (513) 293-8978
M-Sat. 9-6

From Rte. 48 take Kettering exit and head north on Main St. (becomes Far Hills Ave.). Store's on right in Oakwood Plaza.

WORLD OF NATURAL FOODS
8351 North Main St., 45419 • (513) 890-8000
M-F 10-8, Sat. 10-5

From I-70, take Englewood exit (just west of I-75) south on Main St. Store's on right in Randolph Plaza.

KENT
KENT NATURAL FOODS CO-OP
151 East Main St., 44240 • (216) 673-2878
M-Sat. 10-6:30

 Main St. is Rte. 59. Store's one block east of Rte. 43 on north side.

MIDDLEBURG HEIGHTS
AMERICAN HARVEST
13379 Smith, 44130 • (216) 888-7727
M-F 9:30-8:30, Sat. 10-6

From I-71, take Bagley Rd. exit east. Turn left on Pearl and right on Smith. Store's on right in Southland Shopping Center.

TOLEDO
ABUNDANT LIFE CLAUDIA'S
3132 West Sylvania Ave., 43603 • (419) 472-7212
M-F 9-7, Sat. 9-5, Sun. 12-4

From I-495, take Secor Ave. exit north and turn right on Sylvania. Store's on left.

TOLEDO (cont.)
BASSETT'S HEALTH FOODS
3301 West Central St., 43606 • (419) 531-0334
M-F 9:30-9, Sat. 9:30-8, Sun. 11:30-5:30

From I-475, take Secor exit south. Store's on right in West Gate Shopping Ctr., corner of Secor and Central.

BASSETT'S HEALTH FOODS
4315 Heatherdowns • (419) 382-4142
M-Sat. 9:30-8, Sun. 11:30-5:30 same as above.

From I-80/90, take Exit 4 and go north on Reynolds Rd. Turn right on Heatherdowns. Store's on right.

PHOENIX EARTH FOOD CO-OP
1447 West Sylvania Ave., 43612 • (419) 476-3211
M-F 9-7 (Th 'til 9), Sat. 9-6, Sun. 12-5

From north/east side of I-475, take Willis Pkwy exit and follow signs onto Willis. Turn left on Sylvania. Store's on left.

WOOSTER
WOOSTER FOOD CO-OP
247 West North St., 44691 • (216) 264-9797
M-Sat. 10-6

From Hwy 30, take Rte. 3 North exit. Turn right on North St. Store's on left.

YOUNGSTOWN
GOOD FOOD CO-OP
62 Pyatt St., 44502 • (216) 747-9368
M-Sat. 10-6

From I-680, take Market St. (Rte. 7) exit south. Turn left on Pyatt St.

OKLAHOMA

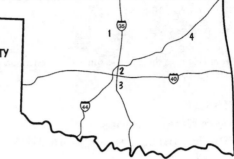

1 ENID
2 OKLAHOMA CITY
3 NORMAN
4 TULSA

ENID
PEARSON'S NATURAL FOOD
Corner of Garriott & Independence, 73701 • (405) 234-5000
Year-round carrots only. Other organic produce seasonal.
M-F 9-5:30, Sat. 9-1

 From I-81, go east on Hwy 412 (Garriott). Store's on right.

NORMAN
EARTH NATURAL FOODS & DELI
309 South Flood Ave., 73069 • (405) 364-3551
M-F 10-7, Sat. 10-6, Sun. 12-5

From I-35, head east on Main St. Turn right on Flood and follow signs to Norman. Store's on left.

OKLAHOMA CITY
AKINS NATURAL FOOD
2924 NW 63rd St., 73116 • (405) 843-3033
M-Sat. 9-9, Sun. 10-6

From I-44, take 63rd St. exit south/west about five miles. Store's on right.

Oklahoma

OKLAHOMA CITY (cont.)

EARTH NATURAL FOODS & DELI
49th & North Western, 73118 • (405) 840-0502
M-F 10-8, Sat. 10-6, Sun. 10-5

From I-244, go three blocks south on Western St. Store's on right in "The Iglesia."

TULSA

AKINS NATURAL FOODS
7801 East 51st St., 74145 • (918) 663-4137
M-Sat. 9-9, Sun. 12-5

From I-44 or 64, turn south on Memorial Drive. Turn right on 51st St. Store's on right in Fontana Shopping Ctr.

AKINS NATURAL FOODS
3321 East 31st St. 74135 •(918) 742-6630
M-Sat. 9-8, Sun. 12-5

From I-44, take Harvard exit north. Turn right on 31st. Store's on left in Newport Square Shopping Ctr.

Dar and Ky Hote at Kerrville Folk Festival – Photo by: Curry Rose Mills

OREGON

1. ASTORIA
2. PORTLAND
3. BEAVERTON
4. SALEM
5. LINCOLN CITY
6. NEWPORT
7. CORVALLIS
8. EUGENE
9. COTTAGE GROVE
10. NORTH BEND
11. GRANTS PASS
12. ROGUE RIVER
13. ASHLAND
14. BEND

ASHLAND
ASHLAND COMMUNITY FOOD STORE
237 North 1st St., 97520 • (503) 482-2237
M-Sat. 8-9, Sun. 10-8

I-5, from south: take Hwy 66 exit, turn left off ramp and take Siskiyow Blvd. Turn right on 1st St. Store's on left. From north: take Valley View exit. Turn right off ramp. Turn left on Hwy 99, which splits and becomes Main (take Main). Turn left on 1st St. Store's on left.

ASTORIA
COMMUNITY STORE
1389 Duane St., 97103 • (503) 325-0027
M-Sat. 10-6

From Hwy 30 (26/101 from south), follow signs to downtown Astoria, and from there, take 12th St. away from river. Turn left on Exchange and left on 14th. Store's on left.

BEAVERTON
NATURE'S FRESH NW
4000 SW 117th St., 97005 • (503) 646-3824
Sun.- Sun. 9-9

From I-5, take Rte. 217 exit and follow signs to Beaverton. Take Canyon exit and turn left on Canyon. Turn right on 117th. Store's on right.

BEND
NATURE'S
1950 NE 3rd St., 97701 • (503) 382-6732
M-F 9:30-9, Sat. 9:30-6, Sun. 11-6

Hwy 97 is 3rd St. Store's on north side inWagner Payless Mall.

DEVORE'S GOOD FOOD
1124 NW Newport, 97701 • (503) 389-6588
M-Sat. 9:30-6:30 (Th 'til 7), Sun 12-6:30

From Hwy 97, go west on Greenwood (becomes Newport). Store's on right.

CORVALLIS
FIRST ALTERNATIVE
1007 SE 3rd, 97333 • (503) 753-3115
M-Sat. 9-9, Sun. 11-8

From I-5, take Hwy 34 exit west into Corvallis. Turn left on 4th St. Store's on left, 8 miles from I-5.

COTTAGE GROVE
SUNSHINE GENERAL STORE
824 West Main St., 97424 • (503) 942-8836
M-Sat. 10-7

From I-5, take Exit 174 and follow signs to Rte. 99. Turn right on Main St. Store's on right.

EUGENE
FRIENDLY FOODS & DELI
2757 Friendly St., 97405 • (503) 683-2079
M-Sat. 8am-10pm, Sun. 9am-10pm

From I-5, take 30th St. exit west towards town. It zigzags twice, becoming 29th, then 28th. Stay on 28th and turn right on Friendly. Store's on right.

KIVA
125 West 11th Ave., 97401 • (503)342-8666.
M-Sat. 9-8, Sun. 10-5

From I-5, take Downtown/Civic Center exit onto 6th Ave. (one way). Turn right on Olive. Store's on right, corner of Olive and 11th Ave.

OASIS FINE
2489 Willamette, 97405 • (503) 345-1014
Sun.-Sun. 8am-11pm

From I-5, take 30th Ave. exit west, turn left on 29th and right on Willamette. Store's on right.

RED BARN
357 Van Buren, 97402 • (503) 342-7503
Sun.-Sun. 9am-10pm

From I-5, take I-105/126 exit west. Take 6th St./Hwy 99 exit and bear right. Turn right on Blair. Store's on right, corner of Blair and 4th.

SUNDANCE NATURAL FOODS
728 East 24th, 97403 • (503) 343-9142
Sun.-Sun. 7am-11pm

From I-5, take 30th Ave. exit and head west. Turn right on Hilyard. Store's on right, corner of 24th and Hilyard.

GRANTS PASS

SUNSHINE NATURAL FOOD MARKET

128 SW H St., 97526 • (503) 474-5044

M-F 9-6, Sat. 10-5

From I-5, take southern Grants Pass exit (of 2) and take Hwy 199 (one direction). Turn right on 7th. Turn left on H St. Store's on right.

LINCOLN CITY

TRILLIUM NATURAL FOODS

1026 SE Jetty Ave., 97367 • (503) 994-5665

M-Sat. 9:30-7

 From Hwy 101, turn east on East Devils Lake Rd. Turn left on Jetty. Store's on right.

NEWPORT

OCEANA NATURAL

213 North Coast Hwy 101, 97365 • (503) 265-8285

Sun.-Sun. 9-7

 Store's on west side of Hwy 101.

NORTH BEND

COOS HEAD FOOD STORE (CO-OP)

1960 Sherman Ave. (Hwy 101 S), 97459 • (503) 756-7264

M-F 9-7, Sat. 10-6, Sun. 12-5

Store's on west side of Hwy 101 S.

PORTLAND

THE DAILY GRIND BAKERY RESTAURANT AND NATURAL FOODS

4026 SE Hawthorne Blvd., 97214 • (503) 233-5521

M-Th 9-9, F 9-3, Sun. 10-7

I-84, from west: take 39th St. exit south. Turn left on Hawthorne. Store's on right. From east: take 43rd St. exit. Turn left at first light. Turn left on 39th. Same as above.

PORTLAND (cont.)

FOOD FRONT CO-OP
2375 NW Thurman, 97210 • (503) 222-5658
Sun.-Sun. 9-9

From I-405, take Rte. 30 exit west. Take Bond St. exit. Turn left on 23rd Place. Store's on right.

NATURE'S FRESH NW
3016 SE Division, 97202 • (503) 233-7374
Sun.-Sun. 9am-10pm (Deli open 2 to 7)

From I-205, take Division St. exit west about 60 blocks. Store's on left.

NATURE'S FRESH NW
6344 SW Capitol Hwy, 97219 • (503) 244-3110
Sun.-Sun. 9am-10pm

From I-5, take Capitol Hwy west. Store's on right in Hillsdale Shopping Center.

NATURE'S FRESH NW
5909 SW Corbett, 97201 • (503) 244-3934
Sun. -Sun. 9-8

From I-205, take any Lake Oswego exit and go south on Macadam St. Turn right on Pendleton. Store's on left, corner of Pendleton and Corbett.

NATURE'S FRESH NW
3449 NE 24th, 97212 • (503) 288-3414.
Sun.-Sun. 9-9

From I-5, take Coliseum exit east on Weidler. Turn left on 24th. Store's on left.

Oregon

ROGUE RIVER
HARMONY NATURAL FOODS & CAFÉ
106 East Main St., 97537 • (503) 582-3075
M-F 9-5:30, Sat. 10-5

From I-5, take Exit 48 and follow signs to Rogue River and northbound, follow signs to store!

SALEM
HELIOTROPE
2060 Market St. NE, 97301 • (503) 362-5487
M-F 9-9, Sat. 9-7, Sun. 10-7

From I-5, take Market St. exit and head west. Store's on left.

SUNRISE MARKET
134 Missouri St. South, 97302 • (503) 375-2105
Sun.-Sun. 8am-9pm

From I-5, take Market exit west. Turn left on Commercial and bear right onto Liberty. Store's on right, corner of Liberty and Missouri.

*The true meaning of quality
encompasses much more than taste.
Quality must include the impact of your endeavor
on the life and environment
of those who grow and process your product,
as well as those who consume it.
At Dean's Beans we combine organic coffee with
activism and progressive development
in the coffee growing villages
to create the highest quality coffee available.*

*Dean Cycon, Co-founder, Coffee Kids,
Roaster of Dean's Beans – (508) 544-3008*

PENNSYLVANIA

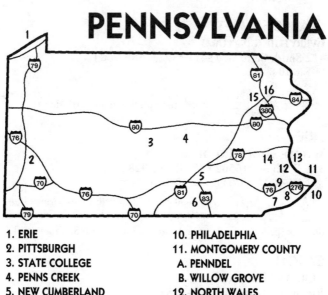

1. ERIE
2. PITTSBURGH
3. STATE COLLEGE
4. PENNS CREEK
5. NEW CUMBERLAND
6. SPRING GROVE
7. WEST CHESTER
8. WAYNE
9. KIMBERTON

10. PHILADELPHIA
11. MONTGOMERY COUNTY
  A. PENNDEL
  B. WILLOW GROVE
12. NORTH WALES
13. NEW HOPE
14. ALLENTOWN/BETHLEHEM
15. CLARKS SUMMIT
16. EYNON

ALLENTOWN

SIGN OF THE BEAR NATURAL FOODS
514 North St. Cloud St., 18104 • (215) 439-8575
M-W 9-7, Th & F 9-8, Sat. 9-5:30

From I-78, take 15th St. exit to Tilghman St. Turn right on Tilghman and left on St. Cloud. Store's on right.

BETHLEHEM

BETHLEHEM FOOD CO-OP INC.
417 Wyandotte, 18105 • (215) 865-1211
Only commercial produce in winter.
M-Sat. 11-5

From I-78, get on 412 N until it ends. Turn left on Wyandotte (I-378). Turn into first parking lot on the left.

CLARKS SUMMIT
EVERYTHING NATURAL
412 South State St. 18411 • (717) 586-9684
M-Sat. 10-8

 Store's right on Rte. 6 on north side.

ERIE
WHOLE FOODS CO-OP
318 E 6th St., 16502 • (814) 456-0282
M-F. 10-5 (Th 'til 7:30), Sat. 10-3:30

From I-90, take I-79 north (becomes Bayfront Hwy). Turn right on State St. and left on 6th. Cut around the park (park divides the street) and continue on 6th St. Store's on left.

EYNON
AURORA NATURAL FOODS
Rte. 6, 18403 • (717) 876-4252
M-Th 10:30-5:30, F 10-8, Sat. 10:30-5

From I-81, take Carbondale exit east. Store's on right. Eynon's near the town of Archibald.

KIMBERTON
SEVEN STARS FARM STORE
West Seven Stars Rd., 19442 • (215) 935-1444
M-F 8-8, Sat. 10-6

I-76, from east: take King of Prussia exit & go west on Rte. 422. Take Rte. 23 exit west & turn left on Rte. 113S. Bear right on Kimberton. Turn right on 7 Stars. Store's on left after covered bridge. From west: take Morgantown exit to Rte. 23. Turn left on Rte. 23. Cross Rte. 100 and go 4 miles. Turn right on Seven Stars. Store's 2 miles down on right.

NEW CUMBERLAND
AVATAR'S GOLDEN NECTAR NATURAL FOODS AND CAFÉ
321 Bridge St., 17070 • (717)774-7215
M & Tu 9-7, W-F 9-9, Sat. 9-5

From Penn. Tpk, take I-83 exit north and take New Cumberland exit. Go east on Simpson Ferry Rd. Turn left on 4th St. and right on Bridge. Store's on left.

NEW HOPE
NEW HOPE NATURAL MARKET
415 B Old York Rd., 18938 • (215) 862-3441
Run by a couple that grows their own organic produce in season!
M-F 9-7, Sat. 10-6, Sun. 1-5

Store's at intersection of Rte. 202 and 179 (Old York Rd.)

NORTH WALES
FRESH FIELDS
1210 Bethlehem Pike, 19454 • (215) 646-6300
M-Sat. 8am-9pm, Sun. 8-8

From Penn. Tpk, take Fort Washington (Rte. 309) exit north.
Store's 3 miles up (on 309) on left.

PENNS CREEK
WALNUT ACRES
Walnut Acres, 17862 • (800) 433-3998
*These acclaimed mail-order organic growers have a store, as well,
and they give tours.*
M-Sat. 9-5, (Winter: Sun. 12-5)

From I-80 go south on Rte. 15, then west on Rte. 45 at Lewisburg.
Take 104 south at Mifflinburg and take first left after Penns Creek
Bridge. Store's on left.

PENNDEL
THE NATURAL FOODS STORE
131 Hulmeville Ave., 19047 • (215) 752-7268
M-Th 10-6:30, F 10-7:30, Sat. 10-5:30, Sun. 11-4

From Rte. 1 (Roosevelt Blvd.), take Penndel exit onto Business Rte. 1
(Old Lincoln Hwy), then "swing off right" on to Hulmeville Ave.
Store's on left.

PHILADELPHIA
ARNOLD'S WAY
4438 Main St., 19127 • (215) 483-2266
M-Sat. 9:30-7 (Tu & W 'til 6), Sun. 11-6

I-76 from east: Take Green Lane and Manyunk exit. Turn right at light and right on Main St. Store's on right. From west: take Roxborough and Manayunk exit, turn left at light, right on Main. Store's on right.

ESSENE, THE NATURAL FOOD MARKET
715-719 South 4th St., 19147 • (215) 922-1146
M-F 9-8, Sat. & Sun. 9-7

From Vine St. Expressway, take Washington/Columbus Ave. exit. Turn west on Christian, right on 3rd and left on Monroe. Store's on right, corner of 4th and Monroe.

PITTSBURGH
EAST END FOOD CO-OP
7516 Meade St., 15208 • (412) 242-3598
M-F 10-8, Sat. 10-6, Sun. 12-5

From I-376, take Edgewood/Swiss Vale exit and follow signs to Edgewood (onto Braddock). Turn left on Meade after Penn Ave. Store's in "The Factory."

SPRING GROVE
SONNEWALD NATURAL FOODS
RD1 Bx 1508, 17362 • (717) 225-3825
A "second generation natural food store."
Tu-Th 10-6, F 10-9, Sat. 8-5

From I-30, head south on Rte. 616 for 2 miles. At York New Salem, turn right at light in the square and go 2 miles to Stoverstown. Store's on right, immediately after cemetery.

WAYNE
FRESH FIELDS
821 Lancaster Ave., 19087 • (215) 688-9400
M-Sat. 8am-9pm, Sun. 8-8

From Penn. Tpk, take I-202 exit south, take Rte. 252 south and head for "Paoli." Turn left on Rte 30 Store's 4 miles up on left.

WEST CHESTER
GREAT PUMPKIN HEALTH FOODS
607 East Market St., 19380 • (215) 696-0741
M-F 9-8, Sat. 9-6, Sun. 10-3

Rte. 3 is Market St. and it's one way. Heading out of West Chester, the store's on the left.

WILLOW GROVE
NATURE'S HARVEST
101 East Moreland Rd., 19090 • (215) 659-7705
M-Th 10-8, F 10-9, Sat. 10-6, Sun. 11-6 (Café open 11:30-4)

From Penn. Tpk., head south on 611. Store's on corner of Rte. 63 and Rte. 611 in Moreland Plaza.

— LISTINGS —

PHILADELPHIA
CENTER FOODS
337 S Broad St., 19107 • (215) 735-5673
Tent. moving in May '94.

STATE COLLEGE
THE GRANARY
2766 West College Ave., 16801 • (814) 238-4844.
Only organic carrots.

RHODE ISLAND

1. PROVIDENCE
2. EAST GREENWICH
3. WESTERLY

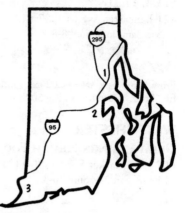

EAST GREENWICH
BACK TO BASICS NATURAL FOOD GROCERY
250 Main St., 02818 • (401) 885-2679
M, T, W & Sat. 10-5, Th & F 10-7, Sun. 12-5

I-95, from north: take Rte. 4 exit and from there take East Greenwich exit. Turn right and go 2.5 miles. Turn left on Main St. From south: turn right off East Greenwich. Take 1st left on Division Rd. Turn left on Main. Store's on right.

PROVIDENCE
BREAD & CIRCUS
259 Waterman, 02906 • (401) 272-1690
Sun.-Sun. 9-9

From I-95, take Rte. 195 exit. Take Exit #3 off I-195 (Gano St.) and turn right at bottom. Turn right on Waterman (2nd light). Store's on right.

WESTERLY
ALLEN'S HEALTH FOOD
Franklin St., 02891 • (401) 596-5569
M-Th 9:30-5:30, F 9:30-6, Sat. 9:30-4

From I-95, take Rte. 78 exit towards ocean/beach. Turn right Rte. 1 (Franklin). Store's on right.

SOUTH CAROLINA

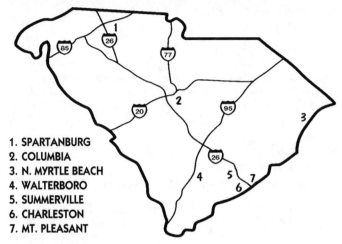

1. SPARTANBURG
2. COLUMBIA
3. N. MYRTLE BEACH
4. WALTERBORO
5. SUMMERVILLE
6. CHARLESTON
7. MT. PLEASANT

CHARLESTON
BOOKS, HERBS, AND SPICES
480 H East Bay St., 29403 • (803) 722-9024
M-F 9-6, Sat. 9:30-5

 *(Store is 2 floors, first floor is W)*

From Hwy 17, take East Bay St. exit and follow signs to East Bay St. Turn right East Bay. Store's on left, across from Channel 5.

RASBERRY'S NATURAL FOOD STORE
1331 Ashley River Rd., 29407 • (803) 556-0076
M-F 9:30-6:30, Sat. 9:30-5:30, Sun. 1-6

From I-26, take I-526 exit. Take Ashley River Rd. South exit. Store's on right, 5 miles down.

COLUMBIA
14 CARROT WHOLE FOODS
2250 Sunset Blvd.West, 29169 • (803) 791-1568
M-Sat. 9-7, Sun. 1-6

From I-20, go east on I-26 to and turn left off Exit 110 (Hwy 378/ Sunset Blvd.). Store's on left in Westland Sq.

COLUMBIA (cont.)

ROSEWOOD MARKET & DELI

2803 Rosewood Dr., 29205 • (803) 765-1083

M-Sat. 9-7, Sun. 1-6

I-26, from south, take Exit 116 to Bluff Rd. Turn left on Bluff and right on Rosewood. Store's on left. From north, take I-77 to 277. Turn left on Calhoun, right on Harden, and left on Rosewood. Store's on left, corner of Rosewood and Maple.

MT. PLEASANT

THE GOOD NEIGHBOR

423 Coleman Blvd., 29464 • (803) 881-3274

M-Sat. 10-6

From I-26S, take Mt. Pleasant exit, but stay in Business Mt. Pleasant. Once you're on the bridge, stay in the far right lane. After 3 lights, turn right into Peach Orchard Plaza.

NORTH MYRTLE BEACH

THE NATURAL FOOD STORE

3320 Hwy 17S, 29582 • (803) 272-4436

M-Sat. 9-8, Sun. 11-5

From Hwy 501, take Rte. 17 Bypass north. Store's on left in Harriss Teeter Shopping Ctr.

SPARTANBURG

GARNER'S NATURAL FOODS

174 Westgate Mall, 29301 • (803) 574-1898

No produce.

M-Sat. 10-9, Sun. 1:30-6

From I-26, head north on US 29. Store's on left, basically at the intersection of these two.

SPARTANBURG (cont.)
GARNER'S NATURAL FOODS
1855 East Main St. (US 29) • (803) 585-1021
Preparing for organic produce.
M-Sat. 9:30-6

From I-26, head north on US 29. Store's on right in Hillcrest Mall.

SUMMERVILLE
GOD'S GREEN ACRE
130 West 3rd North St., 29483 • (803) 873-3953
Organic carrots only.
M-F 10-5, Sat. 10-2

From I-26, take Summerville exit and follow signs to Summerville.
Turn left on Main St. and right on W. 3rd North St. Store's on left.

WALTERBORO
NO JUNK JULIE'S
Rte. 2, Box 49, 29488 • (803) 538-8809
Nutritionist on staff, fun crowd, nice setting.
W & Sat. 9-6, other days by appt. Do call! Julie's great!

From I-95, take Exit 57 towards Walterboro. Turn left on Robertson
Blvd, then left on Hwy 17A north. Bear right at fork in the road. Circle
M Ranch is on the left (w/ red barn). Follow the big carrots to the store.

No Junk Julie

SOUTH DAKOTA

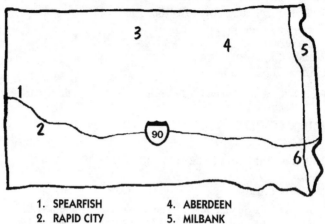

1. SPEARFISH
2. RAPID CITY
3. MOBRIDGE
4. ABERDEEN
5. MILBANK
6. SIOUX FALLS

ABERDEEN

NATURAL ABUNDANCE FOOD CO-OP
114 North Lincoln St., 57401 • (605) 229-4947
M 10-8, Tu- F 10-6, Sat. 10-5

 From Rte. 12, head north on Main St. and turn right on 1st Ave. NE. Turn left on Lincoln. Store's on right.

MILBANK

NATURE'S BEST NATURAL FOOD CO-OP
306 South Main St., 57252 • (605) 432-5614
Tu-Sat. 9-5:30

From Rte. 12, go one block north on Main St. Store's on left.

MOBRIDGE

GOOD NEIGHBOR STORE
217 Main St., 57601 • (605) 845-2097
M-Sat. 9:30-5:30 (Th 'til 9)

Rte. 12 becomes Grand Crossing in Mobridge. Go south on Main St. Store's on right.

RAPID CITY
STAPLE & SPICE MARKET
601 Mt. Rushmore Rd., 57701 • (605) 343-3900
M-F 9-6, Sat. 9-5

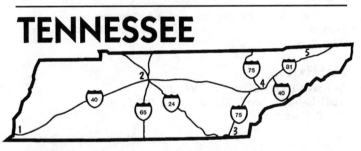

From I-90, take Exit #51 onto Rte. 44 (St. Joe's) south.
Store's on right, corner of St. Joe and Mt. Rushmore.

SIOUX FALLS
EAST DAKOTA FOOD CO-OP
420 1st Ave. South, 57102 • (605) 339-9506
M-Sat. 9-7

From I-29, take 12th St. exit east about three miles.
Turn right on 1st Ave. Store's on left.

SPEARFISH
GOOD EARTH NATURAL FOODS
729 7th St., 57783 • (605) 642-7639
M-Sat. 9-5:30

From I-90, take Jackson Blvd. exit (#12) west 6 blocks. Head
south on 7th. Store's on right.

TENNESSEE

1. MEMPHIS/EAST MEMPHIS   4. KNOXVILLE
2. NASHVILLE   5. ROGERSVILLE
3. CHATTANOOGA

CHATTANOOGA
VITALITY CENTER
1202 Hixson Pike, 37405 • (615) 266-5016
Seasonal organic produce. Carrots year-round.
M-Sat. 9:30-6:30

From I-75, take I-24 spur. Take 4th St. exit (one direction). Turn left on Georgia, then cross over Veterans'
Bridge and continue about a mile. Store's on right.

EAST MEMPHIS
SQUASH BLOSSOM MARKET
5101 Sanderlin Ave., 38117 • (901) 685-2293
M-F 9-9, Sat. 9-8, Sun. 11-6

 Beer only

From I-240, take Walnut Grove exit west into town. Turn left on White Station Rd. and right on Sanderlin. Store's on left in Sanderlin Shopping Ctr.

KNOXVILLE
KNOXVILLE FOOD CO-OP
937 North Broadway, 37917 • (615) 525-2069
M-Sat. 9:30-7:30, Sun. 1-6

 From I-640, take Broadway exit (Rte. 441) south. Store's on right.

MEMPHIS
SQUASH BLOSSOM MARKET
1720 Poplar Ave., 38104 • (901) 725-4823
M-F 9-9, Sat. 9-8, Sun. 11-6 (Deli closes 1 hour early)

Beer Only

From west side of I-240 loop, take Union Ave. exit east. Store's 2 blocks north of Union: overshoot Poplar and double-back on McLean to get to store (no left turn on Poplar from Union).

NASHVILLE
SUNSHINE GROCERY NATURAL FOODS
3201 Belmont Blvd., 37212 • (615) 297-5100
M-F 9-7, Sat. 9-6

From I-440, take 21st Ave. exit into city. Take first right on Sweetbriar and turn right on Belmont at deadend. Store's on right.

ROGERSVILLE
HALLELUJAH ACRES
120 East Main St., 37857 • (615) 272-1800
Run by George Malkmus, author of <u>Why Christians Get Sick</u>.
M-Sat. 10-5

 Store's one block south of 11W, in Rogersville.

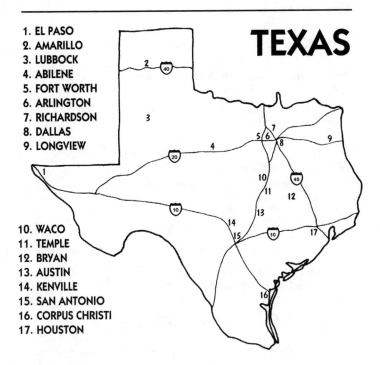

1. EL PASO
2. AMARILLO
3. LUBBOCK
4. ABILENE
5. FORT WORTH
6. ARLINGTON
7. RICHARDSON
8. DALLAS
9. LONGVIEW

TEXAS

10. WACO
11. TEMPLE
12. BRYAN
13. AUSTIN
14. KENVILLE
15. SAN ANTONIO
16. CORPUS CHRISTI
17. HOUSTON

ABILENE

NATURAL FOOD CENTER
2534 South 7th St., 79605 • (915) 673-2726
No organic produce.
M-F 9:30-5:30 (Restaurant: M-F 11-2), Sat. 10-5

From I-20, take Downtown exit and head for south side of Abilene.
Turn left on South 7th. Store's on left.

AMARILLO

EATRITE HEALTH PROMOTION CENTER, RESTAURANT & DELI
2425 I-40 West, 79109 • (806) 353-7476
Organic produce used in snack bar & salad bar.
M-Sat. 9-6

Store's on south side, corner of I-40 and Georgia.

Texas

ARLINGTON
GOOD HEALTH PLACE
2503 South Cooper, 76015 • (817) 265-5261
M-Sat. 9:30-6:30 (Th. 'til 8)

From I-30, take Cooper exit south. Store's on left in Pecan Plaza.

AUSTIN
WHEATSVILLE FOOD CO-OP
3101 Guadalupe, 78705 • (512) 478-2667
Sun.-Sun. 9am-11pm

From I-35, take 38th St. exit west and turn left on Guadalupe. Store's on left.

WHOLE FOODS MARKET
914 North Lamar, 78703 • (512) 476-1206
Sun.-Sun. 9am-11pm

From I-35, take MLK exit west. Turn left on Lamar. Store's on right.

WHOLE FOODS MARKET
4006 South Lamar, 78704 • (512) 448-3884
Sun.-Sun. 9-11

From I-35, take Ben White exit west. Turn left on Lamar. Store's on left.

WHOLE FOODS MARKET
9070 Research Blvd., 78758 • (512) 451-0275
Sun.-Sun. 9am-10pm

From I-35, go north on Hwy 183. Store's on left, corner of Burnet and 183.

BRYAN
SMETANA GROCERY
West Hwy 21, 77803 • (409) 775-9337
M-Th 6am-11pm, F & Sat. 6-midnite, Sun. 7-11

Store's on Hwy. 21, west of Rte. 6, towards Caldwell.

CORPUS CHRISTI
Sun Harvest Farms
1440 Airline, 78412 • (512) 993-2850
Limited seasonal organic produce.
Sun.-Sun. 9-9

 From I-37, take
Padre Island Drive east. Store's on right, corner of Padre & Airline.

DALLAS
Whole Foods Market
2218 Greenville Ave., 75206 • (214) 824-1744
Sun.-Sun. 9am-10pm

From I-75, take Mockingbird Lane exit east. Turn right on Greenville.
Store's on left.

EL PASO
Paso Del Norte Food Co-op
2431 East Yandall, 79903 • (915) 544-0886
Tu, F & Sat. 12-6, W 3-6

I-10, from west: take Cotton Exit and turn left on Cotton, left on
Wyoming, and left on Magnolia. Store's on left, corner of Yandall and
Magnolia. From east: take Cotton exit and turn right on street after
Magnolia, right on Wyoming and left on Magnolia.

FORT WORTH
Cow Town Natural Food Co-op
3539 East Lancaster, 76103 • (817) 531-1233
M-Sat. 10-6

From I-30, take Oakland Blvd. exit south and turn right on
E. Lancaster. Store's on right.

HOUSTON
Whole Foods Market
2900 South Shepherd, 77098 • (713) 520-1937
Sun.-Sun. 9am-10pm

From Hwy 59, take Shepherd/Greenbriar exit and head north on
Shepherd. Store's on left in Alabama Shopping Center.

HOUSTON (cont.)
WHOLE FOODS MARKET
11145 Westheimer, 77042 • (713) 954-3760
Sun.-Sun. 9am-10pm

From I-10, take Wilcrest exit south. Store's on right, corner of Wilcrest & Westheimer in The Market at Westchase.

KERRVILLE
RIVER VALLEY HEALTH FOODS
130-B West Main St., 78028 • (210) 896-7383
M-F 10-6, Sat. 10-5

 From I-10, take either Kerrville exit to Main St. Store's easy to find on Main St. It's two blocks down from HEB Supermarket, and while River Valley has no organic produce, HEB does!

LONGVIEW
JACK'S NATURAL FOOD STORE
1614 Judson Rd., 75601 • (903) 753-4800
M-F 9-6, Sat. 10-5

From I-20, take Estes Pkwy exit north. Estes becomes High St., then Judson. Store's on right, 7 miles up.

JACK'S NATURAL FOOD STORE
2199 Gilmer Rd., 75604 • (903) 759-4262
M-Sat. 9-7

From I-20, take Hwy 259 north, turn left on 281 Loop and left at Gilmer Rd./Hwy 300 exit. Store's on left.

LUBBOCK
THE ALTERNATIVE FOOD COMPANY
2611 Boston Ave., 79410 • (806) 747-8740
Small, mostly seasonal, organic produce section, with plans to expand!
M-Sat. 9:30-6 (Th 'til 7)

 From I-27, take 34th St. exit west. Turn right on Boston. Store's on right.

RICHARDSON
WHOLE FOODS
Coit & Beltline, 75080 • (214) 699-8075
Sun.-Sun. 9am-10pm

From I-75, take Beltline exit and head west. Store's on left, about 2.5 miles out.

SAN ANTONIO
WHOLE FOODS
3711 Colony Drive, 78230 • (210) 696-6331
Sun.-Sun. 9-9

From I-10, take Wurzbach exit. Store's on corner of I-10 and Wurzbach.

WACO
WACO NATURAL FOODS
1424 Lake Air Drive, 76710 • (817) 772-5743
Expanding.
M-Sat. 9-6

From I-35, take Valley Mills Dr. exit north. Turn right on Lake Air Dr. Store's on left.

— *LISTINGS* —

TEMPLE
DISCOVER NATURAL FOODS
1218 South 33rd, 76504 • (800) 373-7783
They're starting to carry organic produce.
M-Sat. 9-6

Photo montage of William and Becky Amsel at Whole Foods, Austin, Texas.
Photo by: Curry Rose Mills

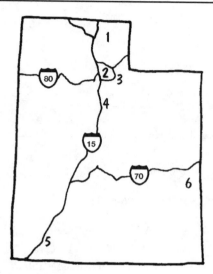

UTAH

1 LOGAN
2 SALT LAKE CITY/ MIDVALE
3 PARK CITY
4 PROVO
5 CEDAR CITY
6 MOAB

CEDAR CITY

SUNSHINE HEALTH FOODS
576 South Main St., 84720 • (801) 586-4889
No organic produce. There's a similar store in St. George (about 50 mi. south).
M-Sat. 10-6

 From I-15, take Rte 14 exit east. Turn south on Main St. Store's on right in Renaissance Square.

LOGAN

STRAW IBIS MARKET AND CAFÉ
52 Federal Ave., 84321 • (801) 753-4777
M-Th 7:30am-11pm, F & Sat. 7:30am-12am, Sun. 10-5

Store is 1/2 block east of Main St. (Rte. 89), and 1/2 block north of scenic Tabernacle Park, on Federal Ave.

MOAB

MOAB COMMUNITY CO-OP
111 North 100 (1st) West, 84532 • (801) 259-5712
Also a bookstore, book-lending space, and gateway to national parks.
M-Sat. 9-6:30 (Winter 9-6)

 Off I-70, go south on Rte. 191. Turn right at first traffic light in Moab (N 1st). Store's right there on left.

PARK CITY
FAIRWEATHER NATURAL FOODS
1270 Iron Horse Dr. 84068 • (801) 649-4561
Only a year and a half old, with plans to grow!
M-F 9-7, Sat. 10-6, Sun. 12-6

From I-80, exit onto Hwy 224 toward Park City Ski Area. Go 5 miles "through suburbia" & turn left on Iron Horse Drive. Store's on left in last store complex.

PROVO
GOOD EARTH NATURAL FOODS
384 West Center St., 84601 • (801) 375-7444
M-Sat. 9-8

From I-15, take Center St. Provo exit east (toward mountains). Store's on left.

SALT LAKE CITY
NEW FRONTIERS NATURAL FOODS
2nd South and 812 East, 84102 • (801) 355-7401
There are 2 stores, same hours, same stuff.
M-Sat. 9-9, Sun. 10-6

Off I-15, take 600S (6th S) exit & head east (toward mountains). Turn left on 800E. Store's at corner of 800E and 200E.

NEW FRONTIERS NATURAL FOODS
2454 S700 East, 84103 • (801) 359-7913
Same hours and info as above.

Off I-80, take 700(7th)E exit. Eastbound, the store's right there, Westbound, go left under the overpass. Store's on right.

— LISTINGS —

MIDVALE
GOOD EARTH NATURAL FOODS (SEE PROVO)
7206 South 900East 84047 • (801) 562-2209

VERMONT

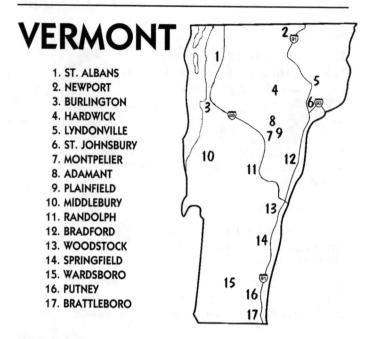

BRADFORD
SOUTH END MARKET
South Main St., 05033 • (802) 222-5701
M-F 9:15-5, Sat. 9-12

From I-91, take Bradford exit. Head east to Rte. 5 and go north on Rte. 5 to Bradford Village. Take a hard left on 25B. Store's on left.

BRATTLEBORO
BRATTLEBORO FOOD CO-OP
2 Main Street, 05301 • (802) 257-1841
M-Sat. 9-8, Sun. 10-6

From I-91, take Exit #1 into Brattleboro, to the end of Canal St. Store's right there, in Brookside Shopping Plaza.

BURLINGTON
ONION RIVER CO-OP
274 North Winooski Ave., 05401 • (802) 863-3659
M-Sat. 9-30-7:30, Sun. 12-5 (closed Sun. in summer)

From I-89, take #14W exit and head west on Main St. Turn right on Union (it ends). Turn right on Winooski. Store's two blocks down on right.

BURLINGTON (cont.)
ORIGANUM
227 Main Street, 05401 • (802) 863-6103
Location may change (for expansion!) in 1994, but phone # will stay the same.
M-F 9:30-7:30, Sat. 9:30-7, Sun. 11-5

Same as Onion River directions, but store's on Main St. on left.

HARDWICK
BUFFALO MOUNTAIN FOOD
Main Street, 05843 • (802) 472-6020
M-Sat. 9-6 (F 10-7), Sun. 10-2

 Main Street is Rte. 15. Store's on east side.

LYNDONVILLE
KINGDOM MARKET
60 Depot, 05851 • (802) 626-3017
M-Sat. 9-5:30

From I-91, take southern Lyndonville exit (of 2). Head north on Rte. 5 about a mile, bear left sharply on Rte. 5 (becomes Depot). Store's on left.

MIDDLEBURY
MIDDLEBURY NATURAL FOOD CO-OP
1 Washington Square, 05753 • (802) 388-7276
M-Sat. 9-7, Sun. 11-5

From Rte. 7, at traffic circle head east on Washington. Store's on left.

MONTPELIER
HUNGER MOUNTAIN CO-OP
403 Barre St., 05602 • (802) 223-6910
M-F 9-7, Sat. 9-6, Sun. 10-4

From I-89, take Montpelier exit onto Memorial. Turn left at Business District sign, onto Main St. Turn right on Barre. Store's on right, about a mile down.

STATE ST. MARKET
20 State St., 05602 • (802) 229-9353
M-F 10-6:30, Sat. & Sun. 10-6

Same as Hunger Mt., but from Main St. turn left on State St. Store's on left.

Vermont ───────────────────────

NEWPORT
NEWPORT NATURAL FOODS
66 Main St., 05855 • (802) 334-2626

Limited organic produce. Opened by brilliant fellow musician, Dana Robinson.
M-Sat. 9-5:30 (F 'til 7)

From I-91, take Downtown Newport exit. At end of access road, turn left on Main St. Store's on right.

PLAINFIELD
WINOOSKI VALLEY FOOD CO-OP
Main St., 05667 • (802) 454-8579
M-F 10-7, Sat. 10-5

 From Rte. 2, go into Plainfield Village. Store's on left, behind fire station.

PUTNEY
PUTNEY CO-OP
P.O. Box 730, 05346 • (802) 387-5866
M-Sat. 7:30am-8pm, Sun. 8-8

From I-91, follow signs to 5 north. Store's on west side of Rte. 5, soon after exit!

RANDOLPH
WHITE RIVER CO-OP
3 Weston Street, 05061 • (802) 728-9554
M-F 10-6, Sat. 9-2

 From I-89, take Exit 4 and take Rte. 66 to Rte. 12S. Weston St. is the first right after the train tracks. Store's on right.

SPRINGFIELD
SPRINGFIELD FOOD CO-OP
76 Chester Rd., 05156 • (802) 885-3363
M-Sat. 9-6, Sun. 12-5

From I-91, take Exit 7 (Springfield). Take Rte. 11 into Springfield, go through town and bear left (stay on Rte. 11). Store's on left.

ST. JOHNSBURY
NATURAL PROVISIONS
93 Portland St., 05819 • (802) 748-3587
M-Sat. 9-5:30, Sun. 11-4

 From I-91, take exit #20 (St. Johnsbury) and take Rte. 5 north. Turn right on Rte. 2. Store's just over Memorial Bridge on the right.

WARDSBORO
NUTSHELL CO-OP
Rte. 100, 05355 • (802) 896-6032
MWF 10-6, Sat. 10-6, Sun. 11:30-4

 Store's on Rte. 100 on the north side.

WHITE RIVER JUNCTION
UPPER VALLEY FOOD CO-OP
49 North Main St., 05001 • (802) 295-5804
M-Th 9-6, F 9-7, Sat. 9-5

 From I-91, take exit #20 (St. Johnsbury) and take Rte. 5 north. Turn right on Rte. 2. Store's just over Memorial Bridge on the right.

WOODSTOCK
EIGHTEEN CARROT NATURAL FOODS
47 Pleasant St., 05091 • (802) 457-2050
M-Sat. 8-6

Pleasant St. is Rte. 4. Store's on east end of Woodstock on south side.

— *LISTINGS* —

ADAMANT
ADAMANT CO-OP
Center Rd./PO Box 1, 05760 • (802) 223-5760

ST. ALBANS
RAIL CITY MARKET
8 South Main St., 05478 • (802) 524-3769
Limited organic produce. Plans to expand.

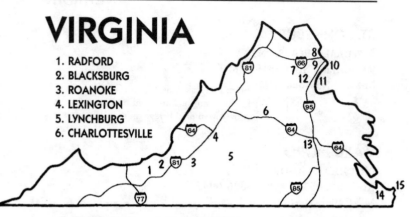

VIRGINIA

1. RADFORD
2. BLACKSBURG
3. ROANOKE
4. LEXINGTON
5. LYNCHBURG
6. CHARLOTTESVILLE

7. WARRENTON
8. FAIRFAX
9. FALLS CHURCH

10. ALEXANDRIA
11. MANASSAS
12. DALE CITY

13. RICHMOND
14. NORFOLK
15. VIRGINIA BEACH

ALEXANDRIA

FRESH FIELDS
6548 Little River Tpk, 22313 • (703) 914-0040
M-Sat. 8-9, Sun. 8-8

From I-395, take Duke St. (# 236) exit west. Duke becomes Little
River Turnpike. Store's on right in Pinecrest Plaza, two miles out.

BLACKSBURG

EATS NATURAL FOODS (CO-OP)
1200 North Main St., 24060 • (703) 552-2279
M-Sat. 9-8, Sun. 12-6

I-81, take southern Christiansburg exit (of 2
exits) to Blacksburg on 460, and take bypass
and exit on Prices Fork Rd. towards downtown. Follow to end. Turn
left on Main St. Store's on right.

ANNIE KAY'S WHOLE FOODS
301 South Main St., 24060 • (703) 552-6870
M-F 9-8, Sat. 9-6, Sun. 12-6

From I-81, take Virginia Tech. exit. Follow signs for
Virginia Tech. onto bypass. Turn north on Hwy 460
to Blacksburg. Take Business District exit onto S. Main. Store's on right.

CHARLOTTESVILLE
INTEGRAL YOGA NATURAL FOODS
923 Preston, 22901 • (804) 293-4111
M-F 9:30-7, Sat. 9-6, Sun. 11-5

 From Rte. 29 (Emmet St.), head east on Barracks Rd. and turn left into Preston

Plaza. Plaza is between Barracks Rd. Shopping Ctr. and Historic District.

FRESH FIELDS
1416 Seminole Trail, 22901 • (804) 973-4900
M-Sat. 9-9, Sun. 9-8

From I-64, take 250 East exit and turn north on Rte. 29 (becomes Seminole Tr.). Store's on left in small shopping center, across from Fashion Square Mall.

DALE CITY
THE NATURAL GROCER
14453 Potomac Mills Rd., 22192 • (703) 494-7287
M-F 10-8, Sat. 10-6, Sun. 12-4

 From I-95, take Exit 156 and follow signs for Potomac Mills. Store's behind Day's Inn Hotel in the Potomac Festival Shopping Center.

FAIRFAX
FRESH FIELDS
5620 Ox Road, 22039 • (703) 503-9000
M-Sat. 9-9, Sun. 9-8

From I-66, take Exit 60 and go south on Rte. 123 to Fairfax for 4.5 miles. Rte. 123 becomes Ox Rd. Store's on right in Fairfax Station Square Shopping Ctr.

FALLS CHURCH
FRESH FIELDS
75 Leesburg Pike, 22043 • (703) 448-1600
M-Sat. 8am-10pm

From I-66, take Rte. 7 (Leesburg Pike) west towards Tyson's Corner. Store's on left, corner of Pimmet Dr. and Leesburg Pike.

FALLS CHURCH (cont.)
KENNEDY'S NATURAL FOODS
1051 West Broad St., 22046 • (703) 533-8484
M-F 10-7, Sat. 10-6

From I-66, head east on Rte. 7. Store's on right in West End Shopping Ctr.

LEXINGTON
HEALTHY FOODS MARKET
110 West Washington St., 24450 • (703) 463-6954
M-F 10-6, Sat. 10-3 (Deli M-F 11:30-3)

From I-81, take Lexington exit, follow signs to Lexington Visitor Center. Pass it. Store's on left.

MANASSAS
HEALTHWAY NATURAL FOODS
10778 Sudley Manor Drive, 22110 • (703) 361-1883
M-Th. 10-7, F 10-8, Sat. 10-6, Sun. 12-5

 From Rte. 66, take Rte. 234 south one mile. Store's on right Bull Run Plaza Shopping Ctr.

NORFOLK
WHOLE FOODS CO-OP
119 West 21st St., 23517 • (804) 626-1051
M-Sat. 10-6

From I-64, take Hwy 264 exit to Norfolk. Stay in left lane and split off towards Waterfront Dr./Downtown Norfolk. Turn right on 21st St. Store's on right.

RADFORD
ANNIE KAY'S WHOLE FOODS
601 3rd. St., 24141 • (703) 731-9498
M-F 9-8, Sat. 9-6, Sun. 12-6

From I-81, take Radford exit. Head towards town on Tyler. Turn left on Norwood (becomes 1st St.) and left on Wadsworth. Store's on right, corner of 3rd and Wadsworth.

RICHMOND
GOOD FOODS GROCERY
1312 Gaskins Road, 23233 • (804) 965-0654
M-Sat. 9-9

From I-64, take Gaskins Rd. South exit about 2.5 miles. Store's on right.

ELLWOOD THOMPSON'S NATURAL. MARKET
4 North Thompson St., 23221 • (804) 359-7525
M-Sat. 9-9, Sun. 11-7

From I-95, take I-195 (Powhite Pkwy) east. Take Cary Street exit.
From north, turn left on Cary and left on Thompson. Store's on left in
a shopping center. (From south, go straight on Thompson).

GOOD FOODS GROCERY
3062 Stony Pt. Rd., 23235 • (804) 320-6767
M-Sat. 9-9

From I-195 South, take the Powhite Pkwy exit, and then the south Forest Hill Ave. exit.
Turn right on Forest Hill Ave. and cross Hugenot Road into Stony Pt. Shopping Ctr.

ROANOKE
ROANOKE NATURAL FOODS
1330 Grandin Rd., 24015 • (703) 343-5652
M-F 9-7, Sat. 9-6, Sun. 1-6

 From I-81, take I-581 South exit, and get
off at 460 west. Turn left on 10th St., right
on Ferdinand, left on 13th St. (becomes Memorial Ave.) and left on Grandin. Store's on left.

VIRGINIA BEACH
THE HERITAGE
314 Laskin Rd., 23451 • (804) 428-0100
M-Sat. 10-7, Sun. 12-6

I-44 ends. Continue straight on 21st St., turn left on Pacific and left on
Laskin. Store's on right.

Virginia

WARRENTON
THE NATURAL MARKETPLACE
5 Diagonal St., 22186 • (703) 349-4111
M-F 9:30-6:30 Sat. 9:30-6

From I-66, take Gainesville/Rte. 29 exit south about 12 miles. Follow signs to downtown Warrenton. Bear right at Business 29 south, go one mile and turn left on Waterloo. Store's on right, corner of Waterloo and Diagonal in light yellow house.

— LISTINGS —

LYNCHBURG
FRESH AIR NATURAL FOODS
3225 Old Forest Rd., 24501 • (703) 385-9252

Tofu Tollbooth researcher Judy Minor and George the Produce Manager pose in spacious **Healthy Pleasures**, in beautiful downtown Manhattan. Photo by: James Sauli

WASHINGTON

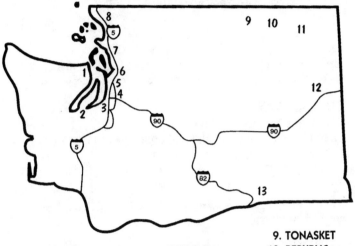

1. PORT TOWNSEND
2. OLYMPIA
3. FEDERAL WAY
4. SEATTLE

5. KIRKLAND
6. EVERETT
7. MT. VERNON
8. BELLINGHAM

9. TONASKET
10. REPUBLIC
11. COLVILLE
12. SPOKANE
13. KENNEWICK

BELLINGHAM
COMMUNITY FOOD CO-OP
1220 North Forest, 98225 • (206) 734-8158
Expanding in April '94.
M-Sat. 9-8, Sun. 11-8

From I-5, take Lakeway exit. Road turns into Holly. Turn left on State St., left on Chesnut and left on Forest. Store's on right.

COLVILLE
NORTH COUNTRY CO-OP
282 West Astor, 99114 • (509) 684-6132
M-F 9-7, Sat. 9-5

Rte. 395 becomes Main St. Turn west on 2nd, left on Wynn and right on Astor. Store's on right.

Washington

EVERETT
South Everett PCC
9121 Evergreen Way, 98204 • (206) 742-1240
Sun.-Sun. 8am-9pm

From I-5, take 128th St. exit and turn left on 128th, right on 4th Ave. and right on 99/Evergreen Way. Store's on right in Anderson Shopping Ctr.

FEDERAL WAY
Marlene's Market & Deli
31839 Gateway Center Blvd. South, 98003 • (206) 839-0933
M-Th. 9-9, F 9am-10pm, Sat. 9-7, Sun. 11:30-6

From I-5, store's right there off the west side of I-5 in Gateway Center (look for blue tile roofs).

KENNEWICK
Highland Healthfood Superstore
101 Vista Way, 99336 • (509) 783-7147
M-Th 9:30-8, F 9:30-3, Sun. 12-5

 From I-82, take Hwy 395 north and turn right on Vista Way. Store's on right.

KIRKLAND
Kirkland PCC
10718 NE 68th, 98033 • (206) 828-4622
Sun.-Sun. 8am-10pm

From I-405, take 70th Place exit (#17) west. Store's on right in Houghton Village Shopping Center.

MT. VERNON
Skagit Valley Food Co-op
202 S. First St., 98273 • (206) 336-9777
M-F 9-7, Sat. 9-6, Sun. 9-4

From I-5, take Kincaid exit west. Turn right on 3rd St. 3rd meets 1st. St. Store's on left.

OLYMPIA
OLYMPIA FOOD CO-OP
921 North Rogers, 98502 • (206) 754-7666
Sun.-Sun. 9-8

From I-5 take Exit 104 to Hwy 101. Take 101 west (only goes one way) and take Black Lake Blvd. exit. Turn right on Black Lake (it changes names along the way). Turn right on Bowman. Store's on corner of Bowman & Rogers.

PORT TOWNSEND
FOOD CO-OP
1033 Lawrence St., 98368 • (206) 385-2885
M-Sat. 9-7:30

From Rte. 20, head into Port Townsend. Road becomes Sims. Turn left on Kearney and right on Lawrence. Store's on right.

REPUBLIC
FERRY COUNTY CO-OP
34 North Clark St., 99166 • (509) 775-3754
M-F 7:30-6, Sat. 10-4

From Rte. 20, turn north on Clark. Store's one block up on right.

SEATTLE
CENTRAL CO-OP
1835 12th Ave., 98122 • (206) 329-1545
Sun.- Sun. 9-9

Coffee just outside store

From I-5, take Denny Way exit east. Store's on right, corner of Denny and 12th.

GREENLAKE PCC
6522 Fremont North, 98103 • (206) 789-7145
M-Sat. 9-9, Sun. 10-7

From I-5, take 50th St. exit west. Turn right on Stone Way, left on West Greenlake Way, right on Linden and left on 66th. Store's on left, corner of 66th and Fremont.

SEATTLE (cont.)

Rainbow Grocery
409 15th Ave. East, 98112 • (206) 329-8440
Sun.-Sun. 9-9

I-5, from south: take Olive Way exit east (becomes John). Turn right as John turns. Turn left on 15th. Store's on left. From north: take Denny Way exit east. Turn left on John. Turn left on 15th. Store's on left.

Ravenna PCC
6504 20th NE, 98115 • (206) 525-1450
Sun.-Sun. 9-9

 *Thinking of expanding in '94.*

I-5, from south: take 65th St. exit east and turn left on 20th. Store's on right. From north: take 80th St. exit and head east on 80th (becomes 75th). Turn left on 65th. Turn right on 20th. Store's on left.

Seward Park PCC
5041 Wilson Ave. South, 98118 • (206) 723-2720
Sun.-Sun. 9-9

From I-405, take Rainier Ave. exit north. Turn right on Seward Park Drive. Store's on left.

View Ridge PCC
6514 40th St. NE, 98115 • (206) 526-7661
Sun.-Sun. 8am-10pm

I-5, from south: take 65th St. exit east to 40th St. Store's on left, corner of 65th and 40th. From north, take 70th St. exit east. Turn right on Roosevelt and left on 65th. Store's on left.

West Seattle PCC
2749 California Ave. SW, 98116 • (206) 937-8481
Sun.-Sun. 8am-10pm

From I-5, take W. Seattle Freeway and from there take the Admiral Way exit. Turn left on California Ave. Store's on right.

SPOKANE
Cedar St. Market (Co-op)
1339 West Main, 99201 • (509) 455-5125
Expanding in '94.
M-Sat. 9-8, Sun. 8-8 (Winter: Sun. 9-8)

From I-90, take Maple St. exit north. Turn right on 3rd Ave., left on Lincoln and left on Main. Store's on left.

Lorien Herbs & Natural Foods
East 414 Trent, 99202 • (509) 456-0702
M-F 10-6, Sat. 10-5

From I-90, Exit 281 (Division) north. Turn right on Trent. Store's on right.

TONASKET
Okanogan River Natural Foods Co-op
21 West 4th St., 98855 • (509) 486-4188
There's a barter fair in October, around the full moon. Ossitta says it's not to be missed!!
M-F 9-5, Sat. 9-6, Sun. 12-4,Winter: M-F 9-6, Sat. 10-5, Sun. 12-4

From Rte. 97 (becomes Main St.), turn west on 4th St. Store's one block down on left.

Curry and Ralph in front of **Wheatsville Co-op**, Austin, Texas - Photo by: Geoffrey Amsel

WEST VIRGINIA

1. HUNTINGTON
2. SPENCER
3. WHEELING
4. MORGANTOWN

HUNTINGTON
THE NATURAL SELECTION
703 West 14th St., 25701 • (304) 525-1644
M 10-6, T-F 10-5, Sat. 10-4

From I-64, take 52 north and turn right at Madison
Ave. exit and left on 14th St. Store's on right.

MORGANTOWN
MOUNTAIN PEOPLE'S CO-OP
1400 University Ave., 26505 • (304) 291-6131
M-F 10-8, Sat. & Sun. 10-6

From I-79, take W.V. Univ. exit towards
Morgantown. Street becomes Beechurst.
Store's on left, at University and Fayette St.

SPENCER
GROWING TREE (CO-OP)
315 Church St., 25276 • (304) 927-3619
M-F 9-5 (closed W), Sat. 9-4

From I-77, take Rte. 33 east 25 miles into town. Turn right
on Church. Store's on left.

WHEELING
TREEFROG GROCERY
2151 Market St., 26003 • (304) 232-0105
M-F 10-5:30, F 10-5, Sat. 10-4 – Store's off of Rte. 70 – *No produce.*

WISCONSIN

1. ASHLAND
2. HAYWARD
3. CUMBERLAND
4. LUCK
5. EAU CLAIRE
6. LA CROSSE
7. GAYS MILLS
8. MADISON
9. BELOIT
10. WAUKESHA
11. MILWAUKEE
12. OSHKOSH

ASHLAND
CHEQUAMEGON FOOD CO-OP
215 Chapple Ave., 54806 • (715) 682-8251
M-Sat. 9-6 (Th 'til 8)

From US Hwy 2, turn south on Chapple. Store's on right, between
2nd and 3rd.

BELOIT
TURTLE CREEK FOOD CO-OP
547 East Grand Ave., 53511 • (608) 365-0975
M-F 10-6, Sat. 10-3

From I-90, take Beloit exit and head west to Hwy 251. Turn north on
Hwy 251 (becomes E. Grand). Store's on right in Hermitage Square
Mall building (same as Rent-a-Center).

Wisconsin ───────────────────

CUMBERLAND
Island City Food Co-op
P.O. Box 152 / 1155 6th Ave., 54829 • (715) 822-8233
M-F 10-5:30, Sat. 10-2

 Store's half a mile southwest of Hwy 63. There's a sign for it on the highway!

EAU CLAIRE
Sunyata Food Co-op & Bakery
409 Galloway St., 54703 • (715) 832-7675
MWF 9-6, Tu & Th 9-7, Sat. 9-5

From Hwy 53, turn west on Main St., right on Farwell St. and left into parking lot, just over bridge.

GAYS MILLS
Kickapoo Exchange Food Co-op
Box 117 / Main St., 54631 • (608) 735-4544
M-Sat. 9-6

 Rte. 171 is Main St. in Gays Mills. Store's on south side.

LA CROSSE
People's Food Co-op
315 5th Ave. South, 54601 • (608) 784-5798
M-Sat. 7am-8pm, Sun. 10-6

From I-90, take Hwy 16 exit south (becomes Losey Blvd.). Turn right on Main St. and left on 5th Ave. Store's on left.

LUCK
Natural Alternatives Food Co-op
241 Main St., 54853 • (715) 472-8084
M, Th, F 10-6, Sat. 10-3

From Rte. 48 head south on Main St. Store's on right.

MADISON
Magic Mill
2862 University Ave., 53705 • (608) 238-2630
M-F 8-9, Sat. & Sun. 9-8

From Hwy 12/18, take Midvale Blvd exit north to its end. Turn right on University. Store's on left in University Station.

Mifflin St. Community Co-op
32 North Bassett St., 53703 • (608) 251-5899
Sun.-Sun. 9-9

From the Interstate that runs along the south of the city, take John Nolan Drive north. Take Broome St. exit north, and turn left on Mifflin St. Store's on left, corner of Mifflin and Bassett.

Williamson St. Food Co-op
1202 Williamson St., 53703 • (608) 251-6776
The famous "Willy St. Co-op"!
Sun.-Sun. 8am-9pm

From John Nolan (see Mifflin directions), bear right. Street becomes Williamson. Store's on left.

MILWAUKEE
Milk-n-Honey Natural Foods
10948 West Capitol Dr., 53222 • (414) 535-0203
M-Th 10-7, F 10-6:30, Sun. 10-5

From Hwy 45, take Capitol Dr. exit (Hwy 190) east one block. Store's on left.

Outpost Natural Foods Co-op
100E Capitol Drive, 53212 • (414) 961-2597
Sun.-Sun. 8am-9pm

From I-43, take Capitol Dr. East exit. Store's on left, about 7 blocks down.

Wisconsin ─────────────────────

OSHKOSH

KITCHEN KORNER HEALTH FOOD
507 North Main St., 54901 • (414) 426-1280
Limited organic produce.
M-Th 9:30-5, F 9:30-6, Sat. 9:30-3

 From Hwy 41, take Hwy 45 exit north and turn left on New York. Turn right on North Main. Store's on right.

WAUKESHA

BITS & PEACE'S FOOD CO-OP
900 Arcadian Ave., 53186 • (414) 544-9130
M-F 10-7, Sat, 10-6

From I-94, take Hwy 18/Waukesha exit to Hwy 164 South and get on Hwy 164. Turn right at 3rd stoplight (no streetsign). Store's on right.

WYOMING

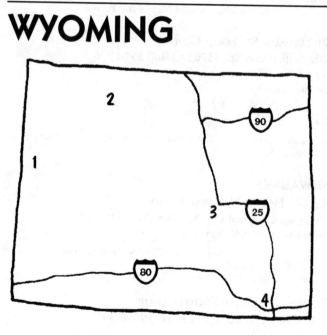

1. JACKSON
2. CODY
3. CASPER
4. LARAMIE

CASPER
BILLIE'S NATURAL FOODS
242 South Wolcott, 82601 • (307) 234-4196
No organic produce.
M-F 9-5, Sat. 9-4

 From I-25, take Center St. exit south. Turn left on Midwest.
Store's on left, corner of Midwest and S. Wolcott.

CODY
WHOLE FOODS TRADING CO.
1239 Rumsey Ave., 82414 • (307) 587-3213
No organic produce.
M-Sat. 9:30-5:30

From Rte. 14 (Sheridan), turn north one block on
Rumsey. Store's on right.

JACKSON
DYNAMIC HEALTH
130 West Broadway, 83001 • (307) 733-5418
Important: this store's name will be changing in 1994!!
M-Sat. 10-6, Sun. 12-5, Summer: M-Sat. 9-8, Sun. 11-6

Rte. 89 is Broadway. Store's on west side.

LARAMIE
WHOLE EARTH GRAINERY
111 Ivinson Avenue, 82070 • (307) 747-4268
Coffee Samples!
Sun.-Sun. 10-6

From I-80, take 3rd St. Exit north. Turn left on Ivinson. Store's on right.

— Notes —

— Notes —

— Notes —

— Notes —

— Notes —